What readers are saying about Jesus Centered

"The writer of Hebrews reminds us that we need to fix our eyes on Jesus so that we can finish the race that God sets before us ... and Steve Brown shows us how! In *Jesus Centered*, Steve's words rekindled my wonder at the thought of being loved by God, refocused my definition of the qualities of a Christ-like leader, and re-energized my passion for introducing others to Jesus."

Paul Borthwick
Jesus follower since 1971, missionary and author

"Steve has written a wonderful resource to help you grow in, up, *and* out! So often, our spiritual formation focuses on our souls *at the expense of* evangelism. In this clear and focused book, Dr. Brown calls leaders to the important and rewarding work of integration! Identity, purpose, calling, formation, and fulfillment all come together in this easily accessible resource. I highly recommend it."

R. York Moore
Executive Director-Catalytic Partnerships,
National Evangelist, Intervarsity,
Author with Gary Chapman of *Seen. Known. Loved.*

"When we were launching Arrow years ago, a leadership specialist asked me to put our vision in one sentence. These words sprang to my mind: 'To help young leaders worldwide to lead to Jesus, like Jesus, for Jesus.' Now Steve Brown has taken this seed thought and expanded it into a book that guides us into precisely that kind of Jesus-centered living and leading. I eagerly welcome and highly recommend this book; may it be widely read and practiced!"

Leighton Ford
Founding President, Leighton Ford Ministries

"Those committed to Jesus-centered living and leading find themselves confronted daily by the weapons of mass-distraction. Steve Brown provides encouragement and practical instruction to find and hold focus, eyes fixed on the author and perfector of our faith: Jesus!"

Commissioner Floyd J. Tidd
The Salvation Army, Territorial Commander for Canada and Bermuda

"This is a welcome reminder of capturing the wonder of Jesus that offers practical steps to make Him the center of our lives and leadership. Steve Brown combines Jesus' story with his own story to invite readers to re-center their lives and to be Jesus-centered leaders. As a Leadership Coach, I really appreciate Steve's very practical and relevant reflection and discussion questions at the end of each chapter, along with the prayers of yielding and worship."

Dr. Ingrid Davis
Leadership Coaching International

"If you, like me, are a Christian leader who is somewhat to very ADHD you will love Steve Brown's core message: Focus! He takes us to the foundation of our relationship with Jesus, helping us to learn from Jesus, the master leader and teacher, and then challenges and coaches us in actually leading lost people to Jesus. Read every chapter, ask every question, pray every prayer ... twice! Your family, your neighbors, and your church will see the impact and be drawn to Jesus."

Dave Brereton
International Director, Youth for Christ International

"The world needs more Jesus-Centered leaders and Steve Brown lights the path forward. Gather some friends around and read this book together. It will help your team take new steps in their faith. You will be blessed by investing the time and effort!"

Rich Birch
Founder, unSeminary

"There is something so foundational to *Jesus Centered* that made it hard to get through the first chapter without a deep wrestling and reflection as a follower of Jesus and a leader of an organization. You will sense a renewed invitation by Jesus that is tender and tangible. Steve points us towards living Jesus-centered lives and leading out of that place; may we all embrace that invitation to see real change!"

Jen Schepens
Director for Envision
(a ministry of the Christian and Missionary Alliance)

"This book has come out during a crazy and unsettling time in our world. At a time like this, we are given the opportunity to make some changes and even reset some areas of our lives. Steve Brown has given some thoughtful insights and practical steps to throw off everything that hinders us in our lives, work, and ministry by centering our identity, motivations, and actions on Jesus. I will be giving a copy of this book to all of our leaders."

Tim Coles
National Director, Youth for Christ Canada

"As a student of leadership, I have been drawn to *identity* as the essence of all true leadership—beyond the mere knowing and doing of leadership. Steve's book is a powerful and timely reminder that being *led by Jesus*, *leading more like Jesus,* and *leading more to Jesus*, is surely the way of receiving and living out the gift and calling of Christian leadership."

Sidney Muisyo
Senior Vice President of Global Program, Compassion International.

"I believe that the first thing a leader must do to make decisions, or at least the 'right' decisions, is to get grounded. Steve Brown has written a sage book for us all, encouraging us to stay grounded on Jesus. Being Jesus-centered matters whether you are leading in your neighborhood, work, home, school, or country. Steve's experience mentoring leaders worldwide, combined with his clear articulation, make *Jesus Centered* an excellent encouragement to stay grounded."

Dr. Carson Pue
Executive Mentor and Founder: Quadrant Group, Author of *Mentoring Leaders: Wisdom for Developing Character, Calling, and Competency*

"What does a surrendered life to Jesus look like? As leaders who are committed to be led more by Jesus, lead more like Jesus, and lead more people to Jesus, we have to be 'all in.' Dr. Steve Brown helps us navigate what it takes to surrender our will, hopes, and preferences because Jesus changes everything. Challenging our preconceived ideas of safety and facing fear, this book is a vital tool for the uncharted ground we are living and leading in today."

Melissa McEachern
Chief Operating Officer, Crossroads Christian Communications Inc.

"Steve Brown is a leader of leaders, not because of a fancy title, but because his life and leadership were tested by the crucible of fire, and he survived to tell the tale. You can't lead others where you haven't been or give to others what you don't have. This poignant and judicious book shows us the way to living Jesus Centered."

Rev. Dr. Sam D. Kim
Co-Founder of 180 Church NYC
Research Fellow, Harvard Medical School Center For Bioethics

"During this season of uncertainty, how do we replace fear with faith, distraction with focus, and the question 'why now?' with 'what's next?' Through this insightful book, Steve shares how the answer is Jesus. If you want to cultivate a renewed wonder at who Jesus is, how he led, and how we can deepen our engagement with him in our life and leadership, this book is a gift."

Michael Messenger
President and CEO, World Vision Canada

**Focusing On Jesus
In A Distracted World**

Jesus Centered

Steve A. Brown

Fedd Books

P.O. Box 341973

Austin, TX 78734

www.thefeddagency.com

Published in association with The Fedd Agency, Inc., a literary agency.

Unless otherwise noted, all scripture quotations are taken from THE HOLY BIBLE, NEW INTERNATIONAL VERSION®, NIV® Copyright © 1973, 1978, 1984, 2011 by Biblica, Inc.® Used by permission. All rights reserved worldwide.

Scripture quotations marked (NKJV) are taken from the New King James Version®. Copyright © 1982 by Thomas Nelson. Used by permission. All rights reserved.

ISBN: 978-1-949784-56-5

eISBN: 978-1-949784-57-2

Library of Congress Control Number: 2020922366

Printed in Canada

First Edition 21 22 23 24 / 4 3 2 1

To Luke, Ainslea, and Lauren

May you always persevere in faith and life by knowing
"Jesus Christ is the same yesterday and today and forever."
Hebrews 13:8

Contents

Opening Prayer

Father God,

Thank You for Jesus. He has no equal and no rival. He is the One and Only. He humbled Himself to enter into human space and skin. He sought Your splendor and glory. He obeyed Your will as a servant and died to bring forgiveness for the sins of the world. He conquered death and is exalted to the highest place. He is Lord of all. He is Lord of me.

Through this book, please stir in me a greater wonder of Jesus and help me focus on Him in a world filled with so many distractions.

My desire is for Jesus to be the center of my life and to center my life on Jesus. Guide me and shape me to be led more by Him, to live and lead more like Him, and to lead more to Him.

I pray these things in the great, the wonderful, and the powerful name of Jesus.

Amen.

Finding Your Focus

**He is before all things, and
in him all things hold together.**

COLOSSIANS 1:17

Sometimes in life we can lose our wonder. It can happen gradually or overnight, but we find ourselves losing awe in something that once captivated us. Our once childlike, wonder-filled outlook begins to dull in light of the familiar.

I remember when I first saw an iPhone. I was amazed by the sleek packaging, stunned by the elegant look, and blown away by the dazzling technology. I was in awe of all it could accomplish. Not only could I call and text on this device, I could email, navigate, google, and even shoot animated angry birds across the digital sky. But then, as time passed, I began to lose my sense of wonder with it. I became distracted by newer and more mesmerizing technology. Now, years later, I view it with the same level of wonder as I view my toaster and sock drawer.

How did this happen? I think that slowly over time, I began to take my iPhone for granted. It became too familiar and my focus drifted elsewhere. Distraction led to dissatisfaction in what once satisfied. What I once embraced with wonder eventually became another helpful tool to accomplish things or entertain myself. It went from the center of my attention to the sidelines of my focus.

Now take Jesus, who is definitely someone to marvel about: do you ever reflect on whether He is at the center or the sidelines of your life? With all the distractions of life competing for your attention, have you lost your wonder of who He is? In our Amazon Prime, short-attention-span culture, we are quick to move from next best thing to next best thing without blinking an eye. Add in the complexity, competing voices, and disruptive change swirling around us and it's easy to be distracted away from Jesus. But when we are not centering our lives on Jesus, we are missing out on *the* best thing: an unparalleled life transformed by the presence and power of the greatest person to ever walk the earth. Despite this, sometimes we lose our wonder of Jesus, or, at least, I do on occasion. I take Him for granted. He becomes too familiar. Our once vibrant relationship becomes transactional. I allow distractions to creep in and I begin centering my life on other things. Before I know it, Jesus is found on the sidelines of my life.

Sound familiar? Can you identify? My goal in writing this book is to help you become captivated afresh by Jesus—and to stay there.

Jesus has no equal. He has no rival. He rises above all. Jesus transcends any and all distractions. He alone is worthy of not just our wholehearted attention but our worship. Only Jesus is God in the flesh. Only Jesus has died for the sins of the world. Only Jesus has conquered death. There are no philosophies, best practices, or fads that can stand up to

Him. There's simply no better example to study. There's no better leader to follow. Jesus lived different. He led different. He's in a league all His own. And yet, Jesus invites you and me into a deep and transformational relationship. He cares about you and wants the best for your life. He wants to be actively involved in every aspect of who you are and what you do. He doesn't want to be treated like a spectator on the sidelines. He desires for your life to be centered on Him where the fulness of His joy can be found.

Jesus being at the center changes everything. This doesn't mean trying your hardest to somehow imitate Him, it's about Christ being formed in you and transforming you from the inside out. Jesus at the center means His character and priorities become your character and priorities.

Philippians 2:5–8 is one passage of Scripture that has helped me to see some of the goals of this radical transformation. You may know this passage well already, but let's look at it again:

> In your relationships with one another, have the same mindset as Christ Jesus: who, being in very nature God, did not consider equality with God something to be used to his own advantage; rather, he made himself nothing by taking the very nature of a servant, being made in human likeness. And being found in appearance as a man, he humbled himself by becoming obedient to death—even death on a cross!

As Jesus willingly entered into a temptation-filled world that focuses on personal gain, He chose to seek God's glory, purposes, and priorities.

In a world that idolizes celebrities, Jesus chose humility. In a world that embraces entitlement, Jesus chose obedience—even unto death. In a world that esteems being served, Jesus chose servanthood.

If you continue reading the passage, you can see how the Father responded to Jesus' unique character and radical choices: "Therefore God exalted him to the highest place and gave him the name that is above every name, that at the name of Jesus every knee should bow ... and every tongue acknowledge that Jesus Christ is Lord, to the glory of God the Father" (vv. 9–11).

The word "every" in these verses stands out to me. Jesus above *every* name. To Jesus *every* knee will bow. *Every* tongue will acknowledge Jesus is Lord.

Jesus desires that His radical ways become your radical ways. He wants humility to be your hallmark. He calls you to obey Him even when there is sacrifice, submission, and suffering involved. He intends for you to serve others. He longs for God's splendor—His glory, praise, and fame—to be your primary focus.

Our world is filled with distractions that may fill your day, but they won't transform your life. When you fix your eyes on Jesus, you never lose your wonder of Him. When you focus with a fresh wonder of Jesus, you will be drawn closer to Him. When you are drawn closer to Jesus, you will be transformed by Him. When you are transformed by Jesus, you will draw others to Him.

Part I

Being Led More by Jesus

Jesus at the center starts with following Him.

1

Follow Him

"Come, follow me," Jesus said,
"and I will send you out to fish for people."

MARK 1:17

Most of the crew were fishermen, and they knew their way around a boat. It was the place they felt most comfortable, but this night was different. There was a storm brewing above and within the water. They found themselves in the midst of it, getting drenched by the powerful waves and hit by the harsh winds. They were desperately searching for land, scanning the horizon for a sign of safety. And then they saw something ... well, they saw someone. Someone was walking on the water.

Assuming they saw a ghost, the disciples became frozen in terror. But as Peter and the rest watched, they realized their Friend was doing the impossible. Jesus' arrival on the scene was an unexpected disruption that was going to change everything.

This wasn't the first disruption Peter witnessed. When Jesus first met Peter, He said three life-changing words to both Peter and his brother Andrew: "Come, follow me" (Matthew 4:19). Those three words were a grand disruption. They had to clear their plans for the day. Fishing was their livelihood, and Jesus wanted them to drop everything to follow Him. They may have even had people waiting to resell their catch. Yet, Peter and Andrew embraced this unexpected disruption. Mark records their response: "At once they left their nets and followed him" (Matthew 4:20). It was an immediate response. Little did they know that this initial decision to follow Jesus would continue to disrupt their lives in ways they couldn't comprehend or imagine.

Choosing to follow Jesus is the starting point for becoming Jesus-centered. The choice is based on an invitation. Notice that Jesus doesn't plead nor force His way with Peter and Andrew. He invites. Peter and Andrew had a choice. The same goes for you and me. Jesus invites you to follow Him. You get to choose your response.

It's important to note that choosing to follow Jesus is not simply a one-time decision. In fact, the invitation to follow Him is an everyday choice. Sometimes it's an every-moment choice, requiring an ongoing response.

●

Following Jesus usually starts with a God-initiated disruption. We have our plans, and we are doing our own thing when God intervenes. The disruption is an invitation to follow Jesus, even though it likely pushes us out of our comfort zone. It's an invitation that usually excludes much explanation and includes many unknowns. The invitation can even seem to include stepping into real danger.

Just think of all the people written about in Scripture who faced God-initiated disruptions and, from there, became history makers and kingdom builders. Moses was tending his father-in-law's flock when he was disrupted by a burning bush (Exodus 3:2). Moses was confronted by God's call for him to lead the Israelites to freedom. Esther was an orphan when her world was first disrupted and she was chosen to be queen, and through her position she saved the Jewish people from the king's decree to exterminate them (Esther 3). Saul (later known as Paul) was on a mission to persecute Christians when a big disruption came. A light from heaven flashed, he heard God speak and went blind (Acts 9). Saul's invitation from Jesus was to make a complete U-turn and embrace His call to spread the same gospel he had been trying to shut down.

And then there was Mary. She was an unmarried teenager whose life was radically disrupted by an angel who told her she would become miraculously pregnant with God's son (Matthew 1). This disruption would have left her with a distraught fiancé, bewildered family, and gossiping community. She would have to process being pregnant with a son who was prophesied to take on David's throne and establish a kingdom that would never end. She would watch this son perform mind-boggling miracles, teach with an authority unlike anyone else, and become the object of rumors, gossip, and hate. She would one day have to watch Him die a horrifying, humiliating, and public death on a cross.

The list could go on and on, but each scenario is similar. It starts with a God-initiated disruption and then an invitation to follow. I can vividly remember a scenario like this that took place in my own life. My wife, Lea, and I were happily settled into a community near family and friends. We were working, serving, and raising our two very small children. Then came a disruption. My boss at the time told me he had come across a job posting that "sounded like me." It's always interesting when your boss suggests you might be better suited for another role, but I trusted him and knew he would be sensitive to what God might be doing. I decided to take a look at the post, and what I saw intrigued me.

The role was with Arrow Leadership, a Christian ministry focused on developing Jesus-centered leaders. I was familiar with the ministry because my own life and leadership had been transformed through their program. However, the job seemed out of my league. Plus, it was 2,500 miles on the other side of the country. I couldn't imagine moving that far from our roots and support system. So, I quickly dismissed the idea out of mind. But just a few days later, I received a call from a mentor. He, too, had seen the same job posting and thought I should consider the role. I couldn't believe it. Now, I had two trusted friends making this suggestion! My initial response was low-level internal panic. I mean, what if Jesus was in this? What if He was inviting me and my family to follow Him across the country? Would I even do well at this job? It seemed like craziness to move that far with two kids under the age of two and no support system to help us.

At this point, I asked God to confirm this was Him asking us to follow. If this was God's invitation, I asked to hear directly from Arrow Leadership's then president, Dr. Carson Pue, figuring this was never going to happen. However, a day or two later, the phone rang. It was Dr. Pue, suggesting I consider the role!

By this point it felt as if Jesus was inviting me to follow Him into a new role, or at least consider it. But it was a disruption that rattled and broke the barriers of my comfort zone. It also confused me. Was this an invitation to faithful obedience or was this foolhardy? Could it be both? I knew that, unlike Peter, we weren't in a boat on raging seas in the middle of the night. But, leaving everything and everyone we knew seemed somewhere between reckless and stupid.

Following Jesus is the first step to becoming Jesus-centered. We are to be followers first. God initiates and His invitation often disrupts our status quo. The ask can seem impossible, foolish, or even dangerous. This is where we must do some discernment and reframing.

When Jesus appeared on the lake, He radically disrupted the chaotic scene of the darkness, wind, and waves in the early morning. To Jesus' words, "Take courage! It is I. Don't be afraid," Peter then asks a question to discern his next steps (Matthew 14:27). He asks, "Lord, if it's you, tell me to come to you on the water" (v. 28). Take note of Peter's words, "Lord, *if* it's you …" Peter is seeking to discern if this is indeed Jesus and not a ghost or his own imagination. Then, Jesus answers, "Come" (v. 29).

Hearing from Jesus doesn't make Peter's decision to follow Him easy. The first step out of the boat is still a huge one. But, through discernment, Peter now knows that this is Jesus. He also knows that if anyone is trustworthy to follow, it is Jesus. This is the same Jesus who first called him and his brother. This is Jesus, the worker of miracles. Peter has seen Him heal the sick—even his own mother-in-law. Peter has witnessed Jesus free people from demons. This is the same Jesus who has led him, taught him, and empowered him to serve. This is the Jesus whose mission is from God.

What or who we follow makes all the difference in the world. Notice how Peter isn't choosing whether or not to follow a philosophy or a belief system. He's called, just like you and me, to follow a person— Jesus. Thankfully, Jesus is in a category all His own. Beloved pastor and theologian John Stott makes this clear by saying, "So we may talk about Alexander the Great, Charles the Great, and Napoleon the Great, but not Jesus the Great. He is not the Great—he is the Only. There is nobody like him. He has no rival and no successor."[1] There's simply nothing and no one better.

To follow, we need to know it's Jesus doing the inviting and calling and not our imagination, our fears, our preferences, or the desires of others. There is a fine line between obedience and stupidity. Sometimes our obedience may seem stupid to others or even to ourselves, but if it is what God has asked us to do, then there is no better thing to do. Other times we may simply do something stupid that is far from what God has asked us to do. The key is discernment.

Which leads me to ask, how do we hear and know God's call? How do we separate God's voice from our own voice or the voices of others? The starting place is to acknowledge that God does speak, and that He can be creative in doing so. Scripture gives examples of God speaking through angels, dreams, signs, and wonders—even the mouth of a donkey. While you may or may not encounter God through these rare forms of revelation, you can hear from God right now through Scripture. The words of the Bible are the very words of God. As 2 Timothy 3:16–17 says, "All Scripture is God-breathed and is useful for teaching, rebuking, correcting and training in righteousness, so that the servant of God may be thoroughly equipped for every good work." Listening to God through Scripture is at the heart of following Jesus and being Jesus-centered.

The first step in listening to God through Scripture is to see if there is explicit direction. Does God say anything about the specific issue or question? If He does, we simply need to obey and follow. If we can't find anything specific, we should look for principles from God's Word that apply to the situation. Principles go beyond a specific question and inform a general approach. For instance, we won't find God's explicit direction on how to deal with a specific person. However, we will find that we should deal with the person in keeping with the principle of love. The bottom line is that we should never take steps that are in opposition to explicit or general principles already made clear in Scripture.

●

My own journey has been filled with actively listening for God and to God. His "still small voice" is best heard when I slow down and engage in silence and solitude (1 Kings 19:12 NKJV). This takes practice and patience. Sometimes I can think I hear one thing, but I need to seek out wise counsel in community and the Holy Spirit to help confirm it. I have learned that, when left on our own, we can unintentionally deceive ourselves. Listening just to our own voice can lead us off base and create an echo chamber that only reinforces our own desires. That's why Proverbs 12:15 says, "The way of a fool is right in his own eyes, but he who heeds counsel is wise" (NKJV).

In Peter's case, seeking discernment helped to confirm that he was seeing and hearing Jesus. After that, he had to make a decision: Was he going to follow Jesus' voice and invitation? Was he actually going to get up, walk to the side of the boat, put a leg over, and step out onto the water? Would he leave the relative safety of the boat and step into the dark—in the midst of raging waves and howling winds—to follow Jesus?

The other disciples were probably used to Peter's awkward and spontaneous actions at this point. They had seen their share of his seemingly stupid missteps. Stepping out of the boat during a storm, however, took things to a whole new level. Some disciples must have been rolling their eyes and shaking their heads. It must have felt as though

Peter was bumbling toward his own drowning. Yet, Peter still made the decision to follow Jesus.

On the surface, Peter was stepping into real and serious danger. The wind, the waves, and the darkness made a strong case for it. This is where we need to reframe our perspective about danger. Our culture craves comfort and idolizes safety. Our prayers are full of requests to "keep us safe." But what if what we see as danger isn't really as dangerous as we think?

To follow Jesus means that Jesus is leading. This also means that He is present with His followers. We aren't somewhere off on our own and apart from Him. Jesus changes everything because He is Immanuel— God with us. What is dangerous in a world where God is with us? If the all-powerful and all-knowing God is with us and even in us, in the form of the Holy Spirit, then shouldn't God's very presence dramatically change our calculus around any danger we may face? Furthermore, if we know our story ultimately ends with a "happily ever after" scenario, shouldn't that change our perspective of worry or doubts about following Jesus? Shouldn't the fact that you have a "living hope through the resurrection of Jesus Christ from the dead, and into an inheritance that can never perish, spoil or fade" (1 Peter 1:3–4) put the perceived danger of following Jesus into perspective?

Spiritual writer Theresa of Avila wrote in the sixteenth century, "In light of heaven, the worst suffering on earth will be seen to be no more serious than one night in an inconvenient hotel."[2] This quote is in no way meant to trivialize or minimize the very real pain and suffering endured by people on this side of heaven. But the key words "in light of heaven" bring an eternal perspective that highlights the unimaginable wonder, beauty, and goodness of heaven, which causes current suffering to become relatively and comparably small. What seems dangerous now will look far different from the perspective of heaven. We weren't put on the planet to seek out comfort: instead, we are called to join in a mission. Being Jesus-centered means being called to live radically and faithfully with God for God's purposes.

There's no getting around the fact that there can also be very real costs to following Jesus. Too often, the picture of following Him is painted with mountaintop moments, perks, and benefits—eternal life is the ultimate benefit. Yet Jesus was clear that following Him had a cost in the here and now. In Luke 9:23 He says, "Whoever wants to be my disciple must deny themselves and take up their cross daily and follow me."

Following Jesus means surrendering our will, our hopes, and our preferences to Him. This surrender is a decision that begins our relationship with Him—and it's an ongoing, everyday decision as we continue to follow Him. Sometimes it's a string of moment-by-moment decisions.

This invitation to "take up your cross and follow me" was as Philip Yancey writes, "the least manipulative invitation that has ever been given."[3] We are allowed to count the cost before surrendering. Sometimes it will involve big things and sometimes little things. Being Jesus-centered means choosing a lifetime of surrendering.

By calling us to surrender, Jesus isn't asking you and me to do something He didn't do himself. In perfect obedience, He surrendered to his Father's will and plans. He submitted to bearing the weight of our sins and drinking the cup of suffering. On a brighter side, Jesus also brought everlasting glory to God and opened the way for God's reconciliation with all of humanity. Jesus' obedient surrender at the cross defeated sin and death, gave access to the kingdom of God, and initiated a revolution that continues two thousand years on. Through His surrender, Jesus is exalted at the right hand of His Father, where every knee will bow and every tongue confess that Jesus Christ is Lord.

Following Jesus requires surrender, but there's a beautiful irony. As Mark 8:35 says, "For whoever wants to save their life will lose it, but whoever loses their life for me and for the gospel will save it." In other words, in God's upside down kingdom economy, the act of surrendering your life actually brings you the *real* life you may be trying to seek. Similarly, the act of not surrendering costs us more than we will ever know.

I remember feelings of fear and danger stirring inside me when I listened to a phone message from a mentor. He invited Lea and me to consider leading a summer mission team to countries that were frequently in the news for being hostile and actively opposed to Christians. I perceived the destinations to be pretty dangerous. So, when I returned the call, I asked my mentor about the "danger factor." His response floored me and changed my perspective. He said, "Steve, it depends on your definition of danger. I think it's far more dangerous for people to stay home in their basements scrolling through media all summer."

Where we think is safe may actually be more dangerous. The boat may have looked safer to Peter, but was a water-logged boat buffeted by the waves *actually* safer than being next to Jesus? No. In the grand scheme of things, by choosing to abandon his boat and follow Jesus' invitation, Peter was in the best place possible.

The decision to follow Jesus will stir your fears. I bet Peter's knees were knocking in fear as he swung his legs over the side of the boat. I bet Esther's hands were shaking with nerves as she walked into the king's court to plead for her people. We know that even the bold and unflappable, super-missionary Paul dealt with "conflicts on the outside, fears within" (2 Corinthians 7:5), so don't be surprised if your knees start knocking. In Peter's case, he began to walk on the water toward Jesus, but when he saw the wind, "he was afraid and, beginning to sink, cried out, 'Lord, save me!'" (Matthew 14:30). In a world filled with distractions and apparent dangers, we need to abide in and keep our eyes focused on Jesus.

Reflection Questions

1. Can you think of a time when you sensed Jesus disrupting your life and asking you to follow Him? Was it an easy or hard decision? How did you respond? How did God respond?

2. What fears stir in you when you consider following Jesus? In the grand scheme of things, why might these fears be unfounded?

3. Like Peter in the boat, what might you be holding onto other than Jesus for security right now? Why? What might the act of holding on to something other than Him be costing you?

4. How does the idea that you are "called to live radically and faithfully with God for God's purposes" inspire or challenge you?

A Prayer

Father God,

By Your grace, as part of being Jesus-centered, I choose to deny myself and pick up my cross and follow You today.

You are my Master. You are the way, the truth, and the life.

Help me to hear Your voice, ground me in Your Word, and gather around me a wise community. Guard me from listening to any voice that opposes Your voice. Guard me from idols of comfort and safety.

Give me the courage to follow You, whatever the mission and regardless of the circumstances or cost.

Remind me that following You means that I am not alone. You are with me and that's the best thing possible.

In the one and only name of my Lord Jesus, I pray these things.

Amen.

2

Abide in Him

"I am the vine; you are the branches.
If you remain in me and I in you,
you will bear much fruit;
apart from me you can do nothing."

JOHN 15:5

Jesus was a master communicator. He often used stories or examples from everyday life to make His point and help people remember His teaching. To truly follow Him and make a difference in the kingdom of God, Jesus taught that His disciples needed to abide in Him the way a branch connects to a vine—if separated, the branch will die. In John 15:5, Jesus says, "I am the vine; you are the branches. If you remain in me and I in you, you will bear much fruit; apart from me you can do nothing." In order to live an abundant and fruitful life, Jesus told His disciples they needed to stay connected to Him as their source of life.

The same is true for us—we can't do things on our own and expect to bear fruit.

It has taken me years to come to grips with the hard truth that I can't contribute *anything* to Jesus' work on the cross. Whatever my attempts at good works, I cannot and, ultimately, could never contribute anything toward righting my relationship with God. I have found there's no other option but to embrace the fact that my salvation was God's work from start to finish.

For some reason, just like my attempts to earn right standing with God, I often think I need to live out the Christian life on my own. I try my best, but I can't find what it takes from within me. Instead, I get stuck, I fail, I reach exhaustion, and I end up really frustrated. As a slower learner, I have come to this conclusion: You can try to follow Jesus in your own strength and power, but you will always come up short. Whatever your level of desire and whatever the intensity of your own willpower, Jesus said, "Apart from me you can do nothing" (John 5:15). There is just no way you can live the Christian life and keep yourself at the center. In trying to do so, you will get stuck, you will fail, you will be exhausted, and you will end up very frustrated.

To be Jesus-centered, we must abide in Jesus. How do we abide? By realizing our utter dependency on Him and relying on Him all day, every day. The starting point is recognizing our complete dependence on God. For most people, this is the main challenge. Our pride inspires us to think we must be able to pull this off on our own. We think that since Jesus did the heavy lifting at the cross, we should be able to take things forward from there. Trying to dig deep and press forward on our own may show short-term signs of success, but the results are always less than they could be with God's power and presence. There is always less positive change, blessing, or noteworthy impact if our effort is based on our personal, limited strength and finite abilities.

Depending on ourselves rather than on God is also unsustainable and harmful. Ajith Fernando, longtime director of Youth for Christ in Sri Lanka, South Asia, put his finger on this as one of the main causes of burnout amongst Christians and leaders. Of this approach, he writes, "We are ministering in our own strength rather than in the Spirit's inexhaustible resources."[4]

Each of us have some responsibility and a role to play in the Christian life. As Philippians 2:12 says, you are to "continue to work out your salvation with fear and trembling." But we can't miss what comes next: "For it is God who works in you to will and to act in order to fulfill his good purpose" (v. 13). In other words, there is a partnership—and when we refuse partnership with God, we have no power. The vine is the life and power source for the branches. Only the vine can bring critical nutrients to the branches. The vine provides and the branches receive. If a branch becomes disconnected from the vine, it will wither and die.

As the vine, Jesus is able to give you strength and power to do all things He has called you to do. The same power God unleashed in your salvation is readily available to you today and every day. The image of the vine and branches isn't just about the availability of God's power; it's also about intimacy. There is a deep, vibrant, and on-going connection between vine and branch. This is God's heart for your relationship with Him. He desires to walk each moment of every day with you.

Living with the power of God at work in and through us brings not only a special intimacy with God but also a special kind of freedom. Jesus makes this very invitation: He says, "Come to me, all you who are weary and burdened, and I will give you rest. Take my yoke upon you and learn from me, for I am gentle and humble in heart, and you will find rest for your souls. For my yoke is easy and my burden is light" (Matthew 11:28–30).

Jesus acknowledges the futility of trying to live apart from His power—we will be weary and burdened. Thankfully, He points to another option—we can learn from His gentle and humble way. And as we yield to Him and His yoke, we will be free of the hardship and weight we weren't meant to carry on our own. His power will provide all we need. Abiding in Jesus isn't a new skill or subject that we can master on our own. Our role is to yield, to trust, and to rest in Christ.

Abiding starts by engaging with Jesus each and every day, from the beginning to the end. This can mean conversation with Him through prayer. A friend of mine starts conversation by lighting a candle that represents Jesus, grabbing a cup of coffee, saying "good morning," spending a few minutes in silence listening to God, writing in a journal, and reading Scripture. Being filled with the Holy Spirit is another practice of abiding. This means choosing to yield to the presence and power of the Holy Spirit in us. It means allowing the Holy Spirit to teach, guide, empower, and transform us. The outflow of the Holy Spirit's work in us is fruit that is produced—namely, the fruit of the Spirit, which is love, joy, peace, patience, kindness, goodness, faithfulness, gentleness, and self-control (see Galatians 5:22–23).

Like Peter, I can quickly get consumed by the wind and waves around me. This is why ongoing prayer is a key practice for living truly dependent on God. These prayers can be very short, informal, and in the moment. In challenging moments, you can pray prayers such as: "God, you are my strength; God, I choose to depend on you; or God, I can't do this on my own, I need your help!" These simple prayers put our trust in God, demonstrate dependence, invite intimacy, and create space for God to do what only God can do.

When we realize our true dependency on Jesus and seize each opportunity we have to walk moment by moment each day with Him, we begin to see the goodness that results from abiding in Christ. The vine doesn't hold back what its branches need, and God won't hold back what we need. Yielding and depending on God through prayer and living with the power of the Holy Spirit changes everything.

Abiding in Christ, living in day-to-day and moment-by-moment dependence are at the heart of centering our lives on Jesus. By doing so, as Scottish pastor and author William Barclay said: "There enters into our helplessness and fatigue a surge of new life," and we are freshly empowered "to do the undoable, to face the unfaceable, and to bear the unbearable."[5]

Reflection Questions

1. Is it easy or hard for you to abide in Christ? Why?

2. How does the truth that the same power required for your salvation is also available every day change your perspective?

3. What benefits are available when you abide in Christ?

4. What are some practical ways you currently seek to abide in Christ? What are some ideas from this chapter that you can apply?

A Prayer

Jesus,

You are my vine. I am your branch. I am in You and You are in me. Thank You that all You are and have is available to me today. I long to walk each moment of this day with You. I don't want to walk on my own today or any day. I long to see that Your work is accomplished in and through me for Your glory. I recognize I can do nothing of lasting value apart from You. Fill me, Holy Spirit, from the tips of my toes to the top of my head. May Your power fill me, transform me, overflow to others, and produce fruit that glorifies only You.

I pray these things in the name of Jesus, the One whose yoke is easy and burden is light.

Amen.

3

Loved by Him

**"As the Father has loved me,
so have I loved you."**

JOHN 15:9

I'll never forget the time a painting made me realize how little I understood God's love for me. *The Last Supper* by painter Jacopo Tintoretto shattered my mental framework for this intimate scene. Up until that point, almost all the pictures I had seen or imagined of *The Last Supper* focused around thirteen sitting men. Like a sports team photo, they were all behind a table facing the camera, so to speak. Jesus sat in the middle, flanked by six men to His right and six to His left. But Tintoretto's painting provided a different perspective. For starters, there were several dozen people in the picture, some of them women. It didn't look symmetrical, nor orderly. Instead, it looked chaotic and busy, like the meal at a family reunion or church potluck. And then there were the top corners of the painting. The top left corner gave a glimpse into the spiritual realm of angels looking down. The top right corner had what looked like a Holy Spirit fire.

As I tried to wrap my mind around the painting, I pondered the questions: "If I were in this picture, where would I be? Would I be right next to Jesus? Would I be at a distance? Would I be talking to Him or to someone else? Where would I be?"

To be honest, I finally determined that I wouldn't even be in the picture. I actually pictured myself outside the building, far from Jesus. Why would I be outside? In my mind, I was outside because I was busy preparing for what Jesus might need me to do next.

My reflection on the painting stunned me. I was faithfully serving. I was faithfully doing. From most perspectives, I'd get high marks on living out the Great Commandments. Yet, I was actually feeling disconnected and far from Jesus.

On the positive side, I was seeking to express my love for God through serving, and I knew I wanted others to experience God's love. But this moment of realization sounded a loud caution. I began to recognize I wasn't doing and serving based on an overflow of God's love for me; instead, my serving was based on a desire to prove myself worthy of God's love. I was doing and serving with the hope of being loved and accepted by God.

From the outside looking in, all seemed well with my soul. But from the inside looking out, my soul was running on empty, and I was in trouble. I knew that in the long run, I couldn't keep giving away what I didn't possess. Not only was I trying to do something inauthentic, I was trying to achieve the impossible. My efforts were like Peter trying to walk on water without the presence and help of Jesus.

Without a deep, personal connection with God's love, I was seeking to serve out of a reservoir that had no refill point. I often wondered if I had "done" enough, so I would push myself to do more. I kept trying to earn my way to God, and I always ended up feeling as though I had fallen short.

Eventually, I recognized I was also doing and serving solo. I was consumed with doing things *for* God. Notice I write "*for* God" not "*with* God." In trying to do things *for* God, I was working on my own. In my mind, God was separate from my doing. He was like a spectator and judge on the outside. That mindset made doing and serving pretty lonely work. God seemed distant, even though I was the one who had intentionally gone off on my own. I didn't understand that God desired to be with me, even when I wasn't doing and serving.

Somehow, I hadn't figured out that God was very capable of getting things done on His own. After all, He had created the heavens and the earth without me, He continues to sustain His creation without me, and He is sovereignly unfolding His eternal plan. Trying to impress God with my limited capacity was simply exhausting and futile. Instead of standing outside that Tintoretto painting, I wanted to be in the picture and next to Jesus, enjoying Him and living each moment with Him.

When Jesus was asked what the greatest commandment was, He simply replied, "'Love the Lord your God with all your heart and with all your soul and with all your mind.' This is the first and greatest commandment" (Matthew 22:37–38). In other words, if you boil down everything in the law and the prophets, this is the most important command. When you take a first look at this greatest command, it is a "doing" command. The word "love" is a verb directing action to love God. The words "with all your heart and with all your soul and with all your mind" describe the comprehensiveness and magnitude of this active love. But there's something else really important to keep in mind: this greatest command isn't the starting place for our activity. This command is rooted in a foundational truth that we too often miss, forget, or dismiss: God loves us.

It's one thing to express love to God, it's another to deeply and fully receive and experience God's love for yourself. Thankfully, I began to encounter Scripture that helped me to see and understand how God loved me unconditionally. In fact, I learned God already loved me, even when I was living life against His ways. Romans 5:8 became a key verse for me. It reads: "But God demonstrates his own love for us in this: While we were still sinners, Christ died for us." The cross is the ultimate demonstration of God's love. Another verse I found was 1 John 4:19: "We love because he first loved us." Both point out God's initiative in the relationship. As St. Augustine said, "By loving the unlovable, you made me lovable." I learned that our love for God needs to first be established in and flow out of God's love for us. This theme is Paul's heart cry in Ephesians 3:17–19:

> And I pray that you, being rooted and established in
> love, may have power, together with all the Lord's holy
> people, to grasp how wide and long and high and deep
> is the love of Christ, and to know this love that sur-
> passes knowledge—that you may be filled to the mea-
> sure of all the fullness of God.

Paul knew that if we could get our heads and hearts around the magnitude of God's love for us, it would radically change us. He knew that if we were filled with God's love, we would supernaturally overflow with love for God and others.

God's love is foundational to living life and living out the greatest commandment. Yet, we usually miss it or end up forgetting this basic truth. Karl Barth, one of the most influential theologians in the twentieth century, was asked to outline the most significant theme in all his learning and millions of published words. He responded that his greatest theological insight were the words to this simple song, "Jesus loves me, this I know, for the Bible tells me so."[6]

These simple and transformational words can too easily get lost in the distractions of life. A negative experience with an earthly father is one of many reasons this may be. Though I very clearly knew of my own dad's love for me, I have met far too many people who can't fathom a legacy of love from their dad—instead, they hold deep and painful wounds. A bad experience with a human father can then be projected onto our spiritual experience with a loving heavenly Father. As a result, people can have trouble receiving God the Father's love in its pure and holy form.

When my son Luke was quite young, we had a routine of having breakfast together every morning. One particular morning, I was in a hurry for an early appointment. I felt as if I didn't have time for breakfast with Luke, so I quietly left the house without waking him. On my way to the car, I remembered it was garbage day and stopped to carry the garbage pails to the curb. That's when I heard the front door open and heard little Luke crying. My dad instinct kicked in, I dropped the garbage pails, and I ran toward him. I scooped him up into my arms, held him tight, and took him inside. He was crying because he wanted to have breakfast with his dad.

We did have breakfast together that morning, and I was late for my appointment, but God had a more important message for me during the drive to work. It was as if he said, "Steve, you know when you heard Luke crying and your response was to drop everything and run to him? Well, that love you have as a father is just a tiny glimpse of my love for you as your Father." I was stunned. I knew I would do anything for any of my kids. To think of God's love for me being even greater was humbling and hard to fathom.

Sharing that special story often stirs people's hearts to a deeper understanding of the Father's love. In fact, one time I watched a young leader break down after hearing the story. Tears were followed by sobs. When I asked what was going on, he replied that his father would never have dropped everything and run to scoop him up. He then shared that his dad was also a pastor.

This story was the start of a journey toward freedom for this young leader. Rather than being constrained and consumed by what he didn't receive from his earthly father, he embraced an eternal epiphany. He realized his experience with his own dad had skewed and distorted his view of God. He then chose to reject this distortion. He embraced the truth that God, in His love, drops everything and runs to embrace His children. Getting a glimpse of God's true and real love for this young leader turned his tears of brokenness into tears of joy.

That kind of epiphany has the potential to transform. To deeply know you are loved by God brings freedom. It brings security. It brings confidence. It becomes a reservoir that fuels serving and loving others in a sustainable way. It changes how a pastor preaches and teaches, how a parent interacts with his or her kids, or even your posture as you walk down the street. Whatever your context, it's a game changer for how you live and engage with others.

Learning to live with God's love at the center of your being is the start to a path of healing. This young leader began to embrace God's love personally. From there, he was able to forgive his own earthly father. He was also able to have a difficult but redemptive conversation with his dad.

It's not surprising that Jesus deeply knew his Father's love. At His baptism, He and everyone else heard the words, "This is my Son, whom I love; with him I am well pleased" (Matthew 3:17). It's important to note that Jesus heard those words *before* He launched into His formal ministry. In other words, the Father's love wasn't based on Jesus' achievements and doing.

My son Luke's middle name is David. The Hebrew root of David is "beloved." When you break down the word "beloved," you see two words—"be" and "loved." Jesus being at the center of your life means, at the core, knowing and receiving God's love. As Henri Nouwen writes, "Being the Beloved expresses the core truth of our existence."[7] Whatever your flaws and foibles, you are beloved in God's eyes. The only question is whether or not you will receive and embrace that truth and hold it at the center of your life.

In order to center our lives around God's love for us—rather than what we can accomplish for God—we need everyday reminders. For example, God has powerfully used music to saturate my soul with His love. He's also used art. For many years, we've hung a print of Rembrandt's *The Return of the Prodigal Son* in our home. It's a visual reminder of God's love as we come and go each day.

Symbols are another way God powerfully expresses His love to me. I often carry in my pocket a small stone with a cross engraved on it as a tactile reminder. Symbols can be visual reminders that make us pause and think and recenter on Him.

Rhythms are also helpful. Sabbath is a weekly rhythm that confronts me with God's love. There is a freedom to rest in God's love that comes with unplugging weekly from work for a set period of time. During Sabbath, I can't earn my way with God or perform for the applause of others.

However, we can easily get caught up on the when and the how of Sabbath. We may even find ourselves trying to practice Sabbath "just right" in order to please God. But, ultimately, Sabbath is a gift from God. It's a reminder that Jesus has provided the way for a relationship with God through His death on the cross. Since Jesus has already done the work, we can turn our focus toward worship, delight, rest, and just being. I've found that the discipline of Sabbath reminds me just to be, and that God still loves me completely even when I don't "do" or "produce."

Jesus wants for you to be right next to Him in Tintoretto's painting. He loves you more than you know or can imagine. You are beloved, so let yourself "be" loved. Enjoying Him, being enjoyed by Him, and glorifying Him is what you were created for. Centering your life on God's love changes everything. It changes you. It changes how you relate to God. It changes how you see yourself. It changes how you love others. Be loved.

Reflection Questions

1. If someone's life is centered on God's love, how might that change them? What differences can it make?

2. Is it easy or hard for you to "be loved" by God? Why or why not?

3. Has your relationship with your earthly father positively or negatively influenced your relationship with God? How?

4. What are some practical steps you have taken or could take to embrace being the "beloved"? What ideas from this chapter could be helpful to you?

A Prayer

Loving Father,

I don't deserve Your love. I can't earn Your love. Yet, You love me.

I sin. I fail. I'm weak. Yet, You love me.

May Your grace help me to know how wide and long and high and deep is the love of Christ.

Transform me by the truth that Your love surpasses understanding.

Over time, fill me with Your love to the measure of all the fullness of God.

Help me to see and experience Your love in special and deeper ways.

Thank You that Your love endures forever.

I pray these things in the loving name of Jesus.

Amen.

Grounded in Him

**And a voice came from heaven:
"You are my Son, whom I love;
with you I am well pleased."**

MARK 1:11

We are often asked questions such as, "What's your name? What do you do? Where do you live?" We're mostly asked about specific parts of our identity. But how would you respond to the question, "Who are you?"

I like to ask this question to the leaders I walk alongside. A lot of them start their answer with what they do for a living and where they work. They share about their title or role in the workplace. Then many get tongue-tied. The reason is because their work has become so all-consuming, they have lost touch with the rest of who they are. In many ways, they have become their business card. They have lost sight of the multifaceted, dynamic, and complex souls they actually are.

When you think about it, you are much more than your work. You are much more than the various roles in your life. You are a composite of a diverse set of factors and interactions. These include when and where you were born, where you live, your ethnicity, your culture, and your family of origin. Add to the list your education, personality, gender, religious connections and beliefs, calling, gifting, skills, work, and life experience. You also need to factor in your age, stage of life, physical, mental, and emotional health, friendships, relationship status, connections, mentors, economic status, and much, much more.

Each of these additional factors is like a puzzle piece to help build a much bigger jigsaw puzzle of your identity. Putting all these puzzle pieces together is complex and challenging, especially when some of your puzzle pieces change in real-time over the course of your life. So, how do you put your puzzle pieces together to see who you really are?

During seminary, I had the privilege of doing an internship with Christian author and travelling speaker Josh McDowell. One of the many benefits of the internship was being able to listen to Josh speak night after night. I vividly remember one of his talks on identity. Josh asked the audience to share their strategy for putting together a jigsaw puzzle. Some people would respond by sharing they would start with the corners and work on the outside frame. Some would start by separating the pieces into piles of similar colors. The majority, however, would use the front cover of the box. The picture on the box provided a guide to help them see the big picture of what they were trying to put together.

Josh then would ask the audience to imagine the wrong box top had been put on their puzzle box. He would ask how it would feel to discover they were using the wrong box top as their guide. By the immediate groans and grumbling, you could tell that people would be very frustrated.

The point behind the illustration is this: you need the right big picture perspective of yourself in order to put together who you really are, the same way you need the right box top to put a jigsaw puzzle together. Society likes to give us many different options for box tops, or perspectives. Some display images of success, fame, money, and notoriety. But these don't provide the right picture—they don't correspond to our *core* purpose and identity. Ultimately, the right box top is the one provided by the creator of the puzzle. In our case, the ultimate Creator of who we are is God. Therefore, the box top God provides is the right one for us to use. This means we need to align the jigsaw pieces of our life with God's intention and view of who we truly are.

Determining what God's box top looks like for you starts with recognizing that the truest thing about you is what God says about you. What He says about you frames everything about you to the core. It gives clarity and context for every piece. Embracing what God says about you moves you away from the frustration of not knowing how a puzzle piece fits. It stops you from trying to force fit puzzle pieces into places they aren't meant to be. Grounding your identity in God's truth gives you confidence and contentment in a world where so many voices try to undermine or question your identity and worth.

If anyone heard voices trying to undermine and question His identity and worth, it was Jesus. As He begins to share and live out His true identity, nobody—not even His own earthly family—really believed Him. After all, people said, "Isn't this the carpenter's son? Isn't his mother's name Mary, and aren't his brothers James, Joseph, Simon and Judas? Aren't all his sisters with us? Where then did this man get all these things?" (Matthew 13:55–56). In other words, they knew where He came from. They knew His family. They already decided they knew who He was.

This meant He couldn't be who He said He was, so their thinking was that He's a liar or maybe He's crazy or worse.

Who Jesus claimed to be was radically offensive. For starters, He claimed to be God. That's blasphemy, which, back then, was punishable by death. His identity claims also stood directly against the established religious, social, and political order. Needless to say, Jesus would pay a huge price for living out His true identity rather than conform to the one others gave Him. He would end up facing direct and unrelenting opposition from all the power brokers of society. They didn't just gossip, mock, tell lies about Him, or try to trap Him—they went even further. They actively sought to ruin His reputation, expel Him from the community, harm Him physically, and, ultimately, kill Him.

Jesus faces another problem in that both His friends and enemies wanted Him to be somebody else. His closest friends—the disciples—wanted Him to setup His ministry in one place, not preach in multiple regions (Mark 1:35-38). They didn't want Him to fulfill His mission by dying on a cross. The ones closest to Jesus were confused about His identity. His arch enemy, the evil one, was most persistent in this quest. He cornered Jesus at His most vulnerable moments by tempting Him to trade who He really was, and His mission for the counterfeit pleasure and power of this world (see Matthew 4).

What would happen if nobody believed you were who you said you were? What if both your friends and enemies wanted you to be somebody else? You would probably feel frustrated, alone, rejected, and even hurt. You would likely long to be accepted. You might be tempted to do whatever you needed in order to fit in, even if that meant softening your words, buckling to the expectations of others, and abandoning your mission.

This is just a glimpse of what Jesus would have faced. Philip Yancey sums it up well: "Jesus' life was defined by rejection. His neighbors laughed at him, his family questioned his sanity, his closest friends betrayed him, and his countrymen traded his life for that of a terrorist."[8]

Ultimately, we know that Jesus stayed true to His identity and mission, and He did so even with the weight of the sins of the world on His shoulders. He did so even when His friends and followers deserted Him and fled. He did so even though He faced a brutal death on the cross that separated Him from God the Father.

One reason why Jesus stayed the course is because He relentlessly embraced those perfectly timed words from God the Father at His baptism: "You are my Son, whom I love; with you I am well pleased" (Mark 1:11). This public affirmation did not flow from Jesus' achievements, because He hadn't even started His public ministry. These words were unconditional. First and foremost, Jesus' true identity was about *whose* He was—God's Son. His true value was grounded in the Father's love. His significance was rooted in God the Father's delight and expressed in God the Father's affirming encouragement.

Just as Jesus had to keep His identity grounded in this truth—what God the Father said about Him—we need to do the same. Otherwise, we become vulnerable to the voices inside and around us. Left unchecked, this vulnerability leads to insecurity. Insecurity keeps us from being all we were created to be and keeps us from living out our gifts and purposes to the fullest.

Have you noticed that there isn't any insecurity in the life and ministry of Jesus? This is because Jesus fully embraced those core jigsaw puzzle pieces of His identity. Time and time again, Jesus represented the opposite of insecurity. He was grounded, confident, and mission focused because He knew the truest thing about Himself was what the Father said about Him.

Even though we may hear what God says about us, we hear a lot of other voices too. Sometimes these voices conflict with God's voice and begin to stir insecurity. My own insecurity button was pushed when I was stepping into a new role. My predecessor was well-known and widely respected, and I began to hear these words from multiple people: "You've got some big shoes to fill." I knew their intentions were well-meaning, but their words weren't at all helpful.

Thinking about how I would fill my predecessor's "big shoes" was adding to the pressure and anxiety I already felt. I was taking on a role I'd never been in before, and it came with significantly more responsibility. I wanted to succeed. I wanted the ministry to succeed. I wanted to prove myself. I had my own high expectations, and now I was beginning to carry even more weight from the expectations of others.

I soon discovered that I couldn't carry this extra weight. If I was going to measure my success by how I met the expectations of others, I knew I'd be in trouble. For starters, if you focus on the expectations of others (or at least your perception of their expectations), you end up taking your eyes off God's call and your true identity. Instead, you put your eyes and focus on trying to please others. Trying to anticipate and then adapt to the changing expectations of others becomes an uphill battle that you have no chance at winning.

Jesus knew about this temptation. He constantly faced the expectations of others and the temptation to please people. Yet, He kept grounded in His true identity and purpose, and remained focused on being obedient to God's call.

Paul knew about this temptation too. In Galatians 1:10 he wrote: "If I were still trying to please people, I would not be a servant of Christ."

In other words, being a servant of God is incompatible with trying to please people. Philosopher and author Os Guinness reminds us that there is only one person to whom we should look: "I live before the Audience of One. Before others I have nothing to prove, nothing to gain, nothing to lose."[9]

I also learned that trying to fill somebody else's shoes simply doesn't work. God had wonderfully gifted, specifically called, and uniquely equipped my predecessor to serve in a role during a particular season. His gifts, calling, and season of leadership were different than mine. Instead of trying to imitate my predecessor, I needed to embrace the special gifts, specific calling, and particular season God had in store for me. In other words, my feet were different. I couldn't wear anyone else's shoes. I needed to wear my own shoes.

I wonder if David had this same epiphany when Saul had him put on his armor to battle Goliath. When David put it on, he could hardly move. There was no way he was going to successfully fight a giant in Saul's armor. Instead, he chose to fight in his own style—with a slingshot and the presence of God (1 Samuel 17:38–40).

The first step to embracing your true identity is to focus on God, not yourself. Let's test this out. Try to fill in the blank: "I'm not _____ enough."

This isn't usually a time-consuming or difficult question for most people. The answers seem to flow with surprising speed and ease. There are multiple possibilities. Here are just a few examples I've heard:

- I'm not old/young enough.
- I'm not wise/educated enough.
- I'm not good-looking enough.
- I'm not experienced/skilled enough.

- I'm not extroverted enough.
- I'm not good/pure enough.
- I'm not strong/courageous enough.

Unfortunately, this list can go on and on. The fill-in-the-blank words may be different from person to person, but the impact is the same. These words can easily become corrosive self-talk in our minds. With enough of this negative self-talk, we can quickly feel inadequate or even disqualified. Then there can be a very real temptation to self-select out and just stay safe on the sidelines.

This was Moses' reality. In Exodus 3, Moses had an encounter with a burning bush. Through this bush—that didn't burn but did talk—God grabs Moses' captive attention. God shares that He's heard and seen the misery of His people under the oppression of the Egyptians. He shares that He has a plan to bring them freedom and blessing. At this point, everything sounds pretty good to Moses. Then, God's plan gets personal.

In Exodus 3:10 God says to Moses, "So now, go. I am sending you to Pharaoh to bring my people the Israelites out of Egypt." When Moses hears that God wants him to lead the exodus, he doesn't think he should or that he even *could* do it. He responds with the identity question we've been focusing on in this chapter. He asks, "Who am I that I should go to Pharaoh and bring the Israelites out of Egypt?" (v.11).

Behind Moses' question, you can sense him filling in the "I'm not _____ enough" blank. After all, it could be easily argued he isn't qualified for this important and dangerous job. Born an Israelite but raised an Egyptian, Moses doesn't fully belong to either group. Then there's the fact that he is a murderer and fugitive being hunted by Pharaoh. Moses is actually in his own exile taking care of sheep in the middle of nowhere—and they aren't even his sheep! With this less than stellar resume and all the negative self-talk that went with it, Moses wants to self-select out and stay safe on the sidelines. Moses understands that on his own, he is not enough. He doesn't have what it takes.

God doesn't argue with Moses about his resumé. Instead, God responds with "I will be with you" (v.12). In other words, God is saying, "Me being with you is better than anything on your resumé. In fact, Me being with you is enough. My character and My presence are your qualification."

Moses isn't buying it; he's still desperate to find a way out. He says to God, "Suppose I go to the Israelites and say to them, 'The God of your fathers has sent me to you,' and they ask me, 'What is his name?' Then what shall I tell them?" (v.13). Moses continues pressing the question, "What's my qualification?" God again makes Moses' qualifications very clear. He says to Moses, "I AM WHO I AM. This is what you are to say to the Israelites, 'I AM has sent me to you'" (v.14). God wants Moses to take his gaze off of himself and off of his own shortcomings (both real and perceived). Ultimately, God wants Moses to place his eyes on God. There's only one way for Moses to obey and follow what God is asking him to do: Moses must take his eyes off himself and place his full confidence in God.

Let's go back to your fill-in-the-blank statement. Has God called you to do something or entrusted something to you? If so, where are your eyes looking? If your confidence comes from looking at yourself, you are in trouble. This kind of trouble is called pride. If your lack of confidence comes from looking to yourself, you are dismissing God's role. In either case, there is a Helper available to you that is much more able. How might your outlook and confidence change if you look to God, His character, and His presence with you?

The starting point to embracing your true identity is looking to God. The second step is to ground your identity in what God has done for you and what He says about you. I encourage you to take a couple of minutes right now to read Ephesians 1:3–14. It tells us where we must ground our identity. In just this one chapter, the list of what God says about us as believers and what Christ has done for us includes:

- We are blessed in the heavenly realms with every spiritual blessing in Christ.
- We are chosen in Him before the creation of the world.
- We are holy and blameless in His sight.
- We are predestined for adoption through Jesus Christ.
- We are redeemed through His blood for the forgiveness of sins.
- We have the riches of God's grace lavished on us.
- We are included in Christ upon hearing the message of truth.
- We are marked in Him with a seal, the promised Holy Spirit.

Now that's an incredible list! And it's just the start of what God has done for you and for me. It's just the tip of the iceberg of the truest things about every follower of Jesus. Based on just this list of statements above, every follower of Jesus is a spiritual billionaire. If we can deeply embrace these truths at the center of who we are, then our identity will be grounded and unshakeable. Our insecurities will be replaced by God's work and God's truth. As pastor and author Tim Keller writes, "If you're that upset with your status with other people, if you're constantly lashing out at people for hurting your feelings, you might call it a lack of self-control or a lack of self-esteem, and it is. But more fundamentally, you have lost touch with your identity. As a Christian, you're a spiritual billionaire and you're wringing your hands over ten dollars."[10]

If God has already made you a spiritual billionaire, what can the world give or take away that makes a difference? What can you earn or even squander that will make a difference? Who God is, what He has done, and who He says you are needs to be the foundation of your identity. When your identity is grounded in Him, you become the best version of yourself. It is the box top that brings true clarity to all the pieces of your identity. Leaning into this truth can be a game changer, and it centers you on Jesus.

Reflection Questions

1. What "box tops" are you tempted to use for your identity puzzle?

2. How did you fill out the "I'm not _____ enough" blank? When does that thinking manifest itself? What are the costs?

3. If God is with you, as He was with Moses, does that change your outlook or confidence? How?

4. Go back over the list of what God says about you from Ephesians 1. What difference do those statements make for you?

5. Are you being weighed down by the expectations of others? Has pleasing others begun to overtake you? How does what God says about you change things?

6. Are you trying to fill somebody else's shoes? Are you trying to wear somebody else's armor? How can you embrace your own shoes and armor?

7. What difference does it make to think of yourself as a "spiritual billionaire"?

A Prayer

Lord,

Forgive me for putting my eyes squarely on myself.

I cannot qualify myself before You in any way.

You are the great I Am. Thank You for all You have done.

My competency comes from You—Your character, Christ's work on the cross, the Holy Spirit's work in me, the gifts You've given me, and Your presence with me.

The truest thing about me is what You say about me.

Guard me from insecurity. Ground me in Your truth.

Focus my eyes on Jesus, the pioneer and perfector of faith.

By Your grace, help me to live today as a humble, grateful, confident, and generous spiritual billionaire.

I pray these things in the name of Jesus, the One in whom my identity is grounded.

Amen.

Part II

Living and Leading More Like Jesus

*Jesus at the center should make
a real difference in how you live and lead.*

5

Think Like Him

**Do not conform to the pattern of this world,
but be transformed by the renewing of your mind.**

ROMANS 12:2

Peter was confused. He had just heard his friend and leader Jesus say that He was going away, that His body would be broken, and that His blood would be spilled. And the next thing Peter knew, soldiers appeared to arrest Jesus. Peter, seeking to defend and honor Jesus, instinctively takes a sword and cuts off an ear of one of the soldiers (John 18:10).

I'm sure (or at least hopeful) you've never cut off someone's ear, but you've probably acted without thinking. We all have. You've said something quickly and hurt someone's feelings. You've acted without consulting your loved ones or you've prioritized your own agenda without realizing how it would affect others. Most of the time, we have good intentions, but we don't put enough thought into our words and actions.

We can end up getting ourselves into trouble, hurting others, or even misrepresenting Jesus.

When Jesus saw what Peter had done, He said, "Put your sword away! Shall I not drink the cup the Father has given me?" (John 18:11). Jesus had already told Peter the plan. He was facing death so that others might live. He was prepared to face His fate; He was ready to be arrested (or as ready as anyone can be). But Peter was not on the same page as Jesus. Peter hadn't aligned his thoughts with Jesus'. And so, Peter reacted by doing the wrong thing.

If we want to center our lives on Jesus, we need to live and lead like Him. The first step of living and leading like Jesus is aligning our thoughts with His thoughts. We need to think like Him. We need to have the same mindset as Christ.

Simply put, a mindset is a set of beliefs, ideas, and attitudes that guide how you think about yourself, others, and the world. How your "mind is set" can have a tremendous impact on how you live and lead.

God created your mind. Can you imagine that there are over forty billion neurons at work right now in our body's most complex organ—the mind! Your mind processes enormous amounts of data in nanoseconds. Your mind is designed to play a critical role in how you relate to God. When Jesus was asked which command is the most important, He responded, "Love the Lord your God with all your heart and with all your soul and with all your mind" (Matthew 22:37). Your mind is central to loving God.

Throughout Scripture, God points to the importance of our minds. In Romans 12:2, Paul writes, "Do not conform to the pattern of this world, but be transformed by the renewing of your mind. Then you will be able to test and approve what God's will is—his good, pleasing and perfect will." The ongoing renewal of your mind is key to becoming more like Christ and living with Jesus at the center of your life. Colossians 3:2 says, "Set your minds on things above, not on earthly things." Jesus was always thinking about things above; He was thinking about the kingdom—and we should aspire to do the same.

Philosopher and writer Dallas Willard echoes the importance of our minds. He writes, "The prospering of God's cause on earth depends upon his people thinking well."[11] He goes on to say, "Bluntly, to serve God well we must think straight; and crooked thinking, unintentional or not, always favors evil. And when the crooked thinking gets elevated into group orthodoxy, whether religious or secular, there is, quite literally, 'hell to pay.'"[12] What goes on in your mind will not only impact how you live and serve, it will impact God's work in the world. Not thinking well can actually contribute to the spread of darkness.

Seeking to think well, stewarding your mind, and developing a biblical mindset will draw you to Jesus and help you to be centered on Him. His mind was and is remarkable. We do well to remember that the greatest thinker in history was Jesus. As Dallas Willard points out:

> We too easily forget that it is the great thinkers who have given direction to the people of Christ in their greatest moments: Paul, John, Augustine, Luther, Calvin, and Wesley, to name a few. At the head of the list is Jesus Christ himself, who was and is the most powerful thinker the world has ever known.[13]

Jesus has the mindset we need to cultivate. As Philippians 2:5 states, "In your relationships with one another, have the same mindset as Christ Jesus." This passage goes on to recount the humility, service, focus, and obedience that marked His mindset.

Jesus' Humility: Jesus "humbled himself by becoming obedient to death—even death on a cross!" (Philippians 2:8). It's simply mind-boggling that the King of kings and Lord of lords would humble Himself by entering human space and skin. It's beyond comprehension that the great heavenly warrior would submit and surrender to a public and humiliating death as a common criminal. He did that for me, for you, and for the world.

Jesus' Service: Despite "being in very nature God … [Jesus] made himself nothing by taking the very nature of a servant being made in human likeness" (Philippians 2:6–7). The only one deserving of worship chose to serve others.

Jesus' Focus: Jesus' foremost desire was to glorify His Father. Even as He faced His own death, His prayer was, "Father, glorify your name!" (John 12:28).

Jesus' Obedience: In Jesus' obedience to death and giving His life as a ransom for many, the holy and true One chose submission, sacrifice, and suffering over independence.

While adopting the mindset of Jesus in all these areas may seem daunting, there are some tangible action steps we can take.

1. Grow Your Vision of God

Pastor and author A. W. Tozer writes, "What comes into our minds when we think about God is the most important thing about us."[14] Paramount to having the mindset of Christ is a big, clear, and full vision of God. John Stott notes, "Nothing is more important for mature Christian discipleship than a fresh, clear, and true vision of the authentic Jesus."[15] When we grow in wonder of God daily, our vision expands. We will not ever be disillusioned by learning more about God. He is perfect; therefore, our wonder of Him will only increase.

How we think about God impacts everything about us. For example, if we believe God is all-powerful, we will call on Him for miracles. If we believe God is all-present, we can trust that God is near. If we believe God is caring and faithful, we will entrust our cares and burdens to Him. The opposites are also true. If we don't see God as all-powerful, we likely won't call on Him. If we don't believe God is all-present, we can feel far from or even abandoned by God. If we don't think God is caring or faithful, then we become afraid and shameful, feeling as though we need to hide from a God who doesn't care.

Our vision of God makes a big difference in how we develop as Jesus followers. As John Stott adds, "For the discipleship principle is clear: the poorer our vision of Christ, the poorer our discipleship will be, whereas the richer our vision of Christ, the richer our discipleship will be."[16] Beyond our own discipleship, our vision of God impacts whether or not we point others toward God. With a big, full, and clear vision of God, we will have confidence and clarity in sharing with others. The opposite is also true. Without a big, full, and clear vision of God, we will struggle with insecurity and have little to share.

Jesus had a big, clear, and full vision of God. Being one with the Father, Jesus knew the Father. Being one with the Spirit, Jesus knew the Spirit. The intimacy of the Trinity provided Jesus with a mindset unlike any other.

One practical way you can seek to grow your vision of God is by studying aspects of His character and attributes. When reading Scripture, ask yourself what the passage teaches about God's character. Try studying the different names of God used in Scripture—they may add a new dimension to your vision of God you hadn't seen before. Try praying a name, characteristic, or attribute of God for every letter of the alphabet. This simple discipline will help you to begin thinking and memorizing the truths about God. If these truths are planted in your mind, they will influence how you live and lead. They will shape your mindset.

2. Feed Your Mind

We live in a post-truth world of "alternative facts." It is assumed that there's no longer objective truth. Instead, you can have your truth and I can have my truth. So, how are we to navigate a world that claims there is no single truth but multiple truths? I believe we need to consistently and intentionally feed our minds with truth and wisdom. Since God is truth and has revealed Himself in Scripture, it makes sense that we start with a steady diet of God's Word.

If you want to be equipped for God's purposes, you need to be saturated by Scripture. It's important to remember Jesus was saturated by Scripture. In His day, this meant being saturated by the Old Testament. Jesus repeatedly quoted Scripture from memory and used Scripture when He was tempted in the wilderness. For each of the devil's three temptations, Jesus responded with God's Word and truth. That the devil quoted Scripture out of context or incompletely to tempt Jesus is a further encouragement for you and me to know God's Word.

Unfortunately, even though our minds desperately crave a steady diet of truth from God, many of us do not have a regular rhythm of feasting on or studying God's Word. The consequences of not enjoying this practice are stark and is only magnified at a time when society has disconnected from any anchor of truth. To engage Scripture on a regular basis, three ingredients are required: a time, a place, and a plan. If you don't have all three of these ingredients, you won't be able to develop a consistent practice and rhythm in experiencing God's Word.

Time: Focus on identifying and setting aside time each day to engage in God's Word. Though it can be any time of day, for many, it is morning. Pulling away in the early morning was part of Jesus' practice (Mark 1:35). The key is to identify and set aside a time that works for you. If you don't identify a specific time, then you may find yourself failing to find time in the midst of already busy days full of distractions, surprises, and pressures.

Place: This is about identifying and setting aside a specific place where you engage God's Word. Sometimes Jesus connected with God in private places, lonely places, or even the sides of mountains (see Luke 5:15-16, 9:18, and Matthew 14:23). Your place could be what works for you. Your bed, kitchen table, a special chair in your living room, your deck, the park, the lunchroom, or your car can all be options. Some people take the Scriptural idea of a prayer closet and even create a special space in their home to connect with God. There is no right answer that fits for everyone. The goal is to have a regular and specific place where you can be focused on God and Scripture.

Plan: If you have a time and a place but no plan, you likely won't find traction. With so much available technology, there are a ton of options for creating a plan to engage God's Word. For instance, you can google "Bible reading plan" or download the YouVersion app. With these tools, you can create a plan based on specific themes or amount of Scripture. You can also join online reading plans with friends. Some people seek to read the entire Bible in a year. This discipline can provide a good overview of all of God's Word. Some people immerse themselves in one key verse for a day or longer to go deeper into God's Word. Some people download a daily guide app such as Lectio 365. There can be creativity and flexibility. The point is to make a plan.

3. Filter Your Mind

Another key to cultivating the mindset of Christ is to guard your mind. You can do this by filtering what comes into it. The speed and accessibility of the internet makes virtually anything and everything available to your mind at the click of a button or scroll of a finger. If we allow garbage to fill our minds, then it shouldn't surprise us when our minds start focusing on unhealthy thoughts and being tempted to act in sinful ways.

Instead, we need to filter what comes into our minds. Philippians 4:8 gives the ultimate guideline for this kind of filter. Paul writes, "Finally, brothers and sisters, whatever is true, whatever is noble, whatever is right, whatever is pure, whatever is lovely, whatever is admirable—if anything is excellent or praiseworthy—think about such things."

How can this verse help you filter your media consumption? At a time when we can easily become desensitized to hearing profanity, seeing unhealthy and unholy images, engaging crude jokes and memes, and internalizing negative thoughts, we need to be vigilant in guarding our minds.

I've found that excessive social media consumption can devour time, distract me, and mess with my mind. I love keeping up with friends and finding new resources online, but I have struggled with finding a balance. Browsing social media posts often gives us the highlight reel of other people's lives. We see others' amazing vacations, endless awards, and selfies with beautiful friends. This is where my mind can begin to compare my current circumstances with the highlight reel I'm watching. Envy, jealousy, loneliness, escape, and even anger can begin to stir in me. We can also easily bump into nasty, rude, and mean-spirited posts. This can stir negativity, cynicism, or worse: reel us into responding in ungodly ways. It may be worth setting and monitoring boundaries on social media.

Beyond the media and social media world, we need to be wise about the people we spend time with. I recently heard someone say, "We become the average of the five people we are around the most." In other words, we become the average of their character, their passion, and their positive or negative influence. Proverbs 13:20 reminds us to, "Walk with the wise and become wise, for a companion of fools suffers harm." This principle is reinforced in many other places in Scripture, including 1 Corinthians 15:33: "Do not be misled: 'Bad company corrupts good character.'" Take a moment to think of the five people you spend the most time with and whether or not it would be beneficial to become the average of those five people.

4. Focus Your Mind

I'm a runner. I know that many people can't understand why anyone would run voluntarily, but, believe it or not, I mostly enjoy running. It's a rhythm that has brought life to me for over thirty years. Running clears my head, stirs creativity, connects me with God, and helps me stay in good physical shape.

Running is also really hard at times. Sometimes it's hard to get up early to run, especially when it's dark, cold, or raining. One of my biggest mental battles came during a half marathon. I was about nine miles into the 13.1-mile race. At this point, I was lagging, and that's when my thoughts turned negative. "You should have trained harder," "You are never going to finish," "You should give up and take the ride of shame to the finish line in a golf cart," and "You are being passed by really slow runners." Those thoughts, needless to say, were less than motivating. Left unchecked, negative thoughts can become a soundtrack that takes on a life of its own and ruins a runner's race.

I knew I needed to shut down these thoughts before they shut me down. I needed to reframe my thinking on positives—such as the finish line! I imagined what it would feel like to cross it. I pictured my family embracing me at the end. I dreamed about the food tent. I envisioned a warm shower at home, followed by a restorative nap. This positive focus got my mind back on track and determined to finish the race—which I'm thankful to say, I did.

Over the years, I have discovered that what we focus our minds on has extreme power over us. Unfortunately, many people focus on what is unhealthy and negative. The results can be crippling or worse. The good news is that we have the power to choose what soundtrack plays in our heads. As Dallas Willard writes, "The ultimate freedom we have as human beings is the power to select what we will allow our minds to dwell upon."[17] I believe we must be much more selective; actually, ruthlessly more selective in what we allow our minds to dwell upon.

In 2 Corinthians 10:5, Paul writes, "We demolish arguments and every pretension that sets itself up against the knowledge of God, and we take captive every thought to make it obedient to Christ." To focus our minds, we need to live out this verse with the authority we have in Christ. When thoughts begin to form a negative soundtrack in our minds, we need to make them obedient to Christ by rejecting them and shutting them down. Then we need to choose to change the soundtrack to something that speaks of God's truth and life.

Your mind is your most powerful organ. How you think impacts how you live and lead. It impacts how you relate to others and impact the world. The humility, service, focus, and obedience found in the mindset of Jesus is key to living and leading with Jesus at the center.

Reflection Questions

1. What words or phrase would you use to describe your mind's current diet?

2. How can you practically cultivate a bigger, fuller, and clearer vision of God? What would happen if you did?

3. Do you have a place, a plan, and a time for engaging God's Word? If not, what could this look like for you?

4. How do you filter what goes into your mind?

5. Is there a soundtrack that keeps playing in your mind? What is it? Does it need to be taken captive and made obedient to Christ?

A Prayer

Lord,

Thank You for the amazing gift of my mind.

May You transform and renew my mind so I will have the mindset of Christ.

To this end, may my vision of who You are be bigger, clearer, and fuller.

Please give me an unquenchable thirst for You and Your Word. Please give me the discipline to meditate and feast on Your Word so it will be a lamp to my feet and a light to my path.

I ask for the wisdom and strength to filter out lies and anything that is contrary to Your goodness from my mind.

In Your power, I choose to take every thought captive and make it obedient to Christ.

May You be glorified by my transformed mind.

I pray these things in the name of Jesus—the greatest thinker in history.

Amen.

6

Serve
Like Him

**And being found in appearance as a man,
he humbled himself by becoming
obedient to death—even death on a cross.**

PHILIPPIANS 2:8

If the God of the universe were to send His only Son into the world, you would expect a grand entrance. You would expect His arrival to be far more significant than the arrival of a Marvel superhero. Yet Jesus doesn't land on the world stage to the glitter and glamour comparable to a Hollywood premiere. Instead, Jesus starts out as something microscopic. As Philip Yancey writes:

> Unimaginably, the Maker of all things shrank down, down, down, so small as to become an ovum, a single fertilized egg barely visible to the naked eye, an egg

that would divide and redivide until a fetus took shape,
enlarging cell by cell inside a nervous teenager.[18]

You would likely expect that God the Father would ensure the pedigree of His Son's earthly caretakers to be of the highest ranking and social
standing. You wouldn't expect God's Son to be born to a teenager living
in poverty amongst an oppressed and powerless people in an obscure
backwater place. Shockingly, Jesus' care and upbringing were entrusted
to simple people who had no access to positions or networks of power.

You would expect that Jesus' name would help Him to stand out
and above all others. Not so. His name came from the name Joshua and
was very common. It would have compared to someone named James
today. You would think that Jesus, living as God incarnate in this world,
would enjoy the most silver of spoons. Yet, there was never a silver spoon.
Instead, Jesus learned a trade, got His hands dirty, experienced hunger,
thirst, sorrow, and knew the feeling of being tired after a long day. You
would anticipate that once Jesus began His formal ministry, His stature
would change. After all, He is beyond royalty—He is the King of kings.
Yet, Jesus travelled by foot, not by chariot. He didn't have a palace, or
even a dedicated home base of operations. Instead of having servants,
He served others. His entourage wasn't the social and power elite, but a
ragtag group of ordinary and often very broken people. Instead of being
self-promotional, He asked people not to tell of His miraculous deeds. A
donkey was His ride into prominence. His death was a public spectacle
of torture. His tomb became a source of outrage, not a public memorial.

God entering the world through Jesus took a very different path
from what anyone would have expected. He took a path of humility.
Philippians 2:6–8 begins to paint the picture of Jesus: "Who, being in
very nature God, did not consider equality with God something to be

used to his own advantage." Fully unpacking these words cannot be done effectively even in very big books of theology. The bottom line is that Jesus embodied all of God's nature but didn't use His position or power to get His own way or further a personal agenda. Instead, "He made himself nothing by taking the very nature of a servant, being made in human likeness" (Philippians 2:7).

The surprises continue. There's the mind-boggling majesty of the Creator expressed as a fragile creation. There's the all-powerful One as a helpless baby, a growing child, and later, a man hanging on a cross. There's the source and sustainer of life becoming hungry, thirsty, and needing to sleep. There's the One who is ultimate truth having to debate the very existence of objective truth. There's the only One worthy of worship on His knees with a towel in hand, serving others by cleaning their dirty feet.

Philippians 2:8 continues: "Being found in appearance as a man, he humbled himself by becoming obedient to death—even death on a cross!" If humility hadn't been fully expressed up until this point, it now goes beyond the extreme. The One able to call down thousands of angels to defend Himself chooses to submit Himself to a squad of soldiers. The sinless One bears the sins and evil of all time. This holy warrior who deserves a crown allows Himself the public and cosmic humiliation of the cross. The One who could command obedience of angels and force submission of humanity chooses to invite and allow people a choice of whether or not to follow Him.

All of these examples are billboards that powerfully illustrate Jesus' remarkable humility. If anyone was entitled to their privilege and could leverage it for their own gain, it was Jesus. Jesus was the smartest, holiest, and most powerful person in every room He ever entered. Yet, by choosing humility, Jesus chose to live and serve in a radically different way.

Throughout Scripture, God is an ardent champion of humility. In James 4:10 we read, "Humble yourselves before the Lord, and he will lift you up." Again in 1 Peter 5:5–6 we are told, "All of you, clothe yourselves with humility toward one another, because, 'God opposes the proud but shows favor to the humble.' Humble yourselves, therefore, under God's mighty hand, that he may lift you up in due time." This is a tall order when the opposite—pride—is so subtle and so enticing.

Unfortunately, the sin of pride is easy to seed, quick to grow, and really hard to contain. As professor and author Mark Buchanan writes, "Pride grows in most soils, most climates. There are few conditions under which it can't survive, even thrive."[19]

God doesn't mince words about pride. There are many examples in Scripture where God vents and gives warning. Proverbs 16:5 doesn't leave much room for ambiguity. It reads, "The Lord detests all the proud of heart. Be sure of this: They will not go unpunished." God's posture toward pride is hard to miss in Proverbs 8:13: "I hate pride and arrogance, evil behavior and perverse speech." Pride places self at the center, rather than Jesus. Pride blinds a person to their true condition before God. As C.S. Lewis writes, "The essential vice, the utmost evil is Pride. Unchastity, anger, greed, drunkenness, and all that, are mere fleabites in comparison: it was through Pride that the devil became the devil. Pride leads to every other vice: it is the complete anti-God state of mind."[20] Pride is the breeding ground for sin.

The end result of pride is disgrace. As Proverbs 11:2 reads, "When pride comes, then comes disgrace, but with humility comes wisdom." Pride is our greatest enemy. John Stott affirms the perils of pride, "At every stage of our Christian development and in every sphere of our Christian discipleship, pride is the greatest enemy and humility our greatest friend."[21]

Similar to our self-promoting, self-exalting, selfie-saturated world today, humility wasn't actually viewed as positive or good in Jesus' day. It was expected for a leader to position themselves above others and even portray themselves as gods. Humility was viewed as weakness or worse. Jesus lived out a radically counter-cultural example. By saying, "For even the Son of Man did not come to be served, but to serve, and to give his life as a ransom for many" (Mark 10:45), Jesus overturned the status quo. By bending down on His knees, taking a towel, and using His hands to wash His disciples' dirty feet, Jesus demonstrated humility and servanthood in a new and revolutionary way. The cross took things to a entirely unparalleled level.

The way of humility is the way of the kingdom of heaven; boasts of accomplishment and self-sufficiency are not. Wielding privilege, protecting position, and leveraging power to advance yourself at the cost of others is not the way of the kingdom of heaven. The disciples were slow learners on this point. They asked Jesus, "Who, then, is the greatest in the kingdom of heaven?" (Matthew 18:1). Jesus responds by saying, "Truly I tell you, unless you change and become like little children, you will never enter the kingdom of heaven. Therefore, whoever takes the lowly position of this child is the greatest in the kingdom of heaven" (vv. 3–4).

How do you and I follow Jesus' example? How do we become like little children? How do we take the same lowly position? We can begin to emulate Jesus' humility and serve as He served by answering these four key questions.

1. Whom are you lifting up?

The foundation of humility is lifting up or exalting God above ourselves. This means acknowledging God's proper place. Our reverence and worship should be reserved for the one and only God who is truly worthy. John the Baptist was in awe of Jesus. He said, "After me comes the one more powerful than I, the straps of whose sandals I am not worthy to stoop down and untie" (Mark 1:7). Clarity around Jesus' identity stirred humility in John. It also gave him freedom and passion to point people to Jesus rather than attempt to win them to himself.

Whatever our education, accomplishments, strengths, connections, and skills, we need to embrace the fact that they don't hold up against the greatness of God. Our exaltation of God should flow from a healthy fear and reverence of Him. This is the foundation for worship, gratitude, and greater dependence. King David's prayer in Psalm 70:5 reminds me about who God is and who I am not: "But as for me, I am poor and needy; come quickly to me O God. You are my help and my deliverer; Lord, do not delay." In this prayer, David recognizes that God is his help and deliverer. Despite being God's chosen servant, as well as David's accomplishments in killing both a lion and a bear with his hands, he acknowledges his desperate need for God. Though David was under great pressure when he prayed this prayer, the practice of praying a similar prayer—whatever our day-to-day circumstances—will reestablish God's rightful place in our lives.

2. How are you serving?

Jesus' humility is vividly expressed and lived out through serving others. When He took a towel to wash the feet of His disciples, He was upending the social norms of His day. A great teacher or Pharisee would never wash or even get near the dirty feet of his students or followers. To take a position of humility to wash commoners' feet while claiming to be a king was impossible for people to comprehend.

Since Jesus left an example of servanthood, our posture should be one of service. The heart behind serving isn't to receive, but to bless. Serving isn't about getting acknowledgment or applause or status, but rather, helping further someone or something beyond our own direct benefit.

There's been much research done on the importance of serving from your strengths. The core idea is that we should major in what we are good at and minor in what we don't do very well. There's a lot of sense to this. You likely want to make your maximum contribution and impact in alignment with how God has wired you. When you serve from your strengths, you are likely noticed and appreciated. However, you can easily find yourself on automatic pilot. You can feel self-sufficient because of your education, experience, and/or skills. If you are not wary, your dependence on your strengths can draw you away from dependence on God.

The comfort zone of our strengths isn't a good incubator for humility. Instead, we must keep moving from our "safe zone" into a "stretch zone" where we can be pushed outside our comfort and the norm. The stretch zone doesn't need to be a "stress zone," but it does need to be a space that keeps our attention, requires focus, pushes us, invites learning new skills and strategies, and, ultimately, stirs greater dependence on God. Spiritual growth is found in the stretch zone.

For example, over the last few years before COVID-19 restrictions, my family and I had been serving monthly with a mobile soup kitchen and food bank. This isn't my natural comfort zone. Rather than leading, I am being led by others. Rather than teaching, I am lifting boxes, sorting food, and providing hospitality. Rather than being front and center, I am one of many low-profile volunteers. Rather than being in a room where my resume and position is held high, my accomplishments are unknown and unnecessary. Rather than being the one with answers, I sometimes find myself tongue-tied. Yet, it is in this space where I find myself depending on God more, learning from those I serve, letting go of pride, and growing in humility.

Another way to grow in humility is to find hidden or secret ways to serve. Can you think of anonymous ways you could serve your family, workplace, community, or even strangers? Is there a "lowlier" task you could do that maybe doesn't feel normal for you? Is there some way you could bless others that nobody else would find out about? Maybe you could secretly clean the toilets at home or empty the trash bins at work? Serving through these types of practices can bless others while growing our humility.

3. Are you asking for help?

Do you find it easy to receive help from others? What about inviting help from others? I don't want to admit how many times and how many miles I have driven in the wrong direction simply because I didn't want to appear lost. My approach has been to backtrack, rather than humbling myself to invite help. My pride has gotten in the way more than a few times. Many people today find asking for help to be awkward.

Interestingly, Jesus asked for help. Despite the fact that He is the living water and told His disciples that He had "food to eat that you know nothing about," Jesus asked the woman at the well for a drink of water (John 4:32). He received help from the woman who poured the alabaster jar of expensive ointment over His head to prepare Him for His burial (Matthew 26:7). Despite not needing it, He invited the help of His disciples over and over.

When we invite or receive help, precious gifts become available to us. The help of others breeds humility and combats pride. It reminds us that we are not self-sufficient. Our vulnerability can deepen relationships. We need others. Our best response when we have a need is to invite help from others. When someone wants to help you, receive it with thanksgiving.

4. Are you extending help?

The story of the Good Samaritan vividly illustrates humility. A man is suffering on the side of the road, and the people who should be quick to help him are quick to make excuses for why they can't. Then someone the suffering man might have looked down on—an enemy of sorts—passes by and extends a helping hand. The Samaritan ends up providing for all of the injured man's needs by finding him shelter and paying for all of his expenses in the process.

Are you, like the Good Samaritan, going out of your way to extend help toward those in need? When we share our resources—whether time, money, or energy—with someone in need, we are following Christ's example. Jesus would often stop what He was doing, walk miles, even lose sleep to help someone in need. Are you willing to do the same?

●

Despite Jesus' royal pedigree, humility was at the heart of His life and ministry. Whatever your pedigree, heritage, skills, or resume, to center your life on Jesus you are called to follow His example and serve like Him. By doing so, your life will run counter to the culture, lives will change, you will be blessed, and you will bring glory to God.

Reflection Questions

1. Does Jesus' level of humility surprise you? If so, how?

2. How would you view Jesus differently if He were not humble?

3. On a scale of one to ten (ten being *wow*!!) what is your level of awe with who God is and what He has done? How do you think this relates to your level of humility?

4. When and where does pride most often manifest itself in you? Why?

5. What strengths can you leverage for serving God and others?

6. Is it easy for you to ask for help? What blessings come from asking for help?

7. What helps and hinders you to act like the Good Samaritan?

A Prayer

Awesome God,

I desire to walk humbly with You.

Show me any areas of pride in my life and help me uproot them.

Focus my heart on exalting You above all.

May my posture be one of seeking to serve.

Free me to invite Your help and the help of others.

Use me to serve and bless others for Your glory.

I pray these things in the name of Jesus, the King who humbly came to serve.

Amen.

7

Respond Like Him

**Consider him who endured such
opposition from sinners,
so that you will not
grow weary and lose heart.**

HEBREWS 12:3

The Bible is full of examples where people find themselves at a crossroads. They are forced to choose between a path of caution and fear, and a path of boldness and courage.

I suspect Ananias' knees were knocking when he followed God's call to reach out to a blinded Saul, a notorious persecutor of Christians (see Acts 9). Ananias was called to personally give him a message from God. Despite the obvious danger involved, Ananias chose obedience, and he walked in courage.

I'd bet Nathan's mouth was dry with anxiety when he launched into his rebuke of King David's infidelity and murder. But Nathan obediently followed a prophet's calling and confronted David with power. Nathan chose courage.

Day after day, Jesus faced incredible and sustained resistance. There were endless, needy crowds. There were cleverly laid traps to avoid and subtle temptations to resist. His disciples were slow learners and frequent on-the-job sleepers. He endured loneliness and profound internal distress. He had little time to eat or rest. Eventually everyone deserted Him and fled. The culmination of His mission would mean separation from His heavenly Father and bearing the dark deeds of all history. His death would involve great suffering and the public spectacle of crucifixion. Yet, Jesus always chose to respond with courage.

Tim Keller provides a powerful perspective on both the uniqueness of Jesus as well as His constant response of courage. He writes:

> Despite being absolutely approachable to the weakest and broken, he is completely fearless before the corrupt and powerful. He has tenderness without weakness. Strength without harshness. Humility without the slightest lack of confidence. Unhesitating authority with a complete lack of self-absorption. Holiness and unending convictions without any shortage of approachability. Power without insensitivity.[22]

To say that Jesus' mission was difficult is a great understatement. As Jesus prayed and pondered the culmination of His mission at the cross, His anguish reached the point of shedding tears of blood in the garden of Gethsemane. In following Jesus' life through Scripture, we shouldn't be surprised when He promises challenges ahead for His followers. He tells

His disciples in John 16:33, "In this world you will have trouble." There's no lack of clarity there. Trouble is a promise, not merely a possibility.

Dietrich Bonhoeffer reminds us that "the cross means rejection and shame as well as suffering."[23] Despite our longing for the idols of safety and comfort, we shouldn't expect, as students, to be above our teacher. Paul knew suffering well. In 2 Corinthians 11:23–28, Paul lists some of the hardships he endured for the sake of following Jesus. Here goes:

> I have worked much harder, been in prison more frequently, been flogged more severely, and been exposed to death again and again. Five times I received from the Jews the forty lashes minus one. Three times I was beaten with rods, once I was pelted with stones, three times I was shipwrecked, I spent a night and a day in the open sea, I have been constantly on the move. I have been in danger from rivers, in danger from bandits, in danger from my fellow Jews, in danger from Gentiles; in danger in the city, in danger in the country, in danger at sea; and in danger from false believers. I have labored and toiled and have often gone without sleep; I have known hunger and thirst and have often gone without food; I have been cold and naked. Besides everything else, I face daily the pressure of my concern for all the churches.

If Paul's experience does anything, it should reinforce the reality that following Jesus is and will be hard. The question is how will we respond? With fear or with courage? My best working definition of spiritual courage is choosing to follow Jesus, even when your knees are knocking. Breaking this definition down, take note that courage is a choice. We can choose to follow Jesus or not to follow Jesus. Following Jesus means we are being obedient to Him and what He wants us to do. Following Jesus also means we are not alone. If we are following Jesus, then He is very much with us and ahead of us, leading, guiding, providing, and protecting.

When our knees begin knocking, let it be a reminder that courage is not the absence of fear but pressing on in spite of it. Spiritual courage isn't about completely eliminating feelings of fear. Instead, spiritual courage is, by God's grace, choosing to trust, obey, and depend on God in the face of fear.

Living with Jesus at the center of your life requires a courageous response. Courage can be a game changer and world changer. It's hard to underestimate the importance of courage. As C.S. Lewis wrote, "Courage isn't simply one of the virtues, but the form of every virtue at the testing point."[24] In other words, when we are facing fear, feeling overwhelmed, or stretched to the breaking point, we have a choice in our fight. With God's grace, we can choose courage.

Almost everyone needs courage in some area of their life. Maybe you need courage to boldly speak up or to be quiet and listen. Courage to faithfully step forward, to patiently wait, or to graciously step back. Courage to say yes, or no, or not now. Courage to dream or try a new idea. Courage to risk, to obey, or to keep pressing on. Courage to take a stand or to invite help. Courage to reach out or to confront.

Whatever your need today, Jesus provides us with the best example of how to respond with courage in the midst of life's most difficult circumstances. Responding with courage rather than fear is hard, but by God's grace, we can make that choice.

Choose to Walk toward the Light

Keeping your eyes focused on shortcomings and negatives will drain your courage. There will always be problems and places where you can see the negative. If you choose to camp there, you will lose your courage edge.

In Old Testament days, the practice of celebrating and remembering God's work was common tradition. When God did something significant, people would name that place or erect a memorial altar. The purpose was to celebrate and to create tangible reminders of God's faithfulness, power, provision, and protection. The names and memorials also became an educational tool for future generations. When a young person asked about the pile of rocks, they would then hear and be encouraged by a story of God's provision and protection.

We have lost touch with this meaningful tradition of naming places or creating tangible reminders of God's provision and faithfulness. This has come at a cost to our courage, but we can counter this loss through some simple disciplines. Just taking time to make a list of what we've seen God do in the past and what is going well in our lives now can breed thankfulness and courage. Reflect on big and even little wins. This is an exercise that can change your perspective, reset your attitude, help you walk toward the light of Jesus, and fuel your courage going forward. Recording and looking back over these lists can not only restore courage for you but also build courage for those around you.

Choose to Fix Your Eyes on Jesus

Where do your eyes focus when difficulties arise? It's easy to focus on your failures or the shortcomings of others. It's easy to join Peter and focus on the howling wind and the pounding waves. Like the Israelites, we can become paralyzed by "Goliath-sized" problems. But there is another option. You can choose to fix your eyes on Jesus, who has endured and overcome. As Hebrews 12:1–2 says, "Let us run with perseverance the race marked out for us, fixing our eyes on Jesus, the pioneer and perfecter of faith. For the joy set before him he endured the cross, scorning its shame, and sat down at the right hand of the throne of God."

When we fix our eyes on Jesus during difficult times, we are emboldened by His presence. We are encouraged by His example. We are empowered by His strength.

Choose to Lean into Community

Going solo is dangerous even at the best of times. When you are in difficult times, you can choose to lean out of community or lean into community. Leaning out of community leads to isolation and insecurity. Leaning into community brings deeper connection, strength, and, ultimately, courage.

Keeping your feelings isolated internally rarely breeds courage, life, or anything positive. If you are struggling with fears or negative thinking, then identify a safe friend who can listen, encourage, and challenge you in the way of truth. Share how you are feeling, your current challenges, and then pray together.

Remember that Jesus chose to live, love, lead, serve, and suffer in the context of community. He chose to do so even when His community was far from perfect.

Choose to Care for Yourself

Every preflight safety announcement tells you to put on your own oxygen mask before trying to help others; otherwise, you may not have the oxygen you need to actually help anyone else. Though it seems right to focus first on serving and helping others, there's great wisdom in first caring for yourself in healthy, restorative ways. If you don't, not only will your courage edge slowly become dull, but you may bring harm to yourself.

The level of your physical energy is directly linked to your emotional energy. Physical and emotional energy can impact your courage. In fact, General George S. Patton said, "Fatigue makes cowards of us all."[25] If you are feeling flat, fearful, or lacking courage, it may simply be that you are tired and physically depleted. This can be a short-term one-time event, or you can get into cycles and patterns of depletion. Do what you have to do to get caught up on sleep for a few nights. Take some days away if possible. Look for any unhealthy patterns that recur and address them.

Over the course of writing this book, these choices have become very real to me. On top of the COVID-19 pandemic, my wife Lea was diagnosed with breast cancer, so this season was difficult in many ways. All the unknowns, uncertainty, and treatments were particularly challenging. Day by day we had to walk in courage and hope, clinging to the truth. At the very beginning of this journey, I vividly remember sitting in the treatment room waiting for the doctor to come in and share the results of Lea's biopsy. It was a surreal and sobering few minutes before we heard the words, "Lea, you have cancer." Many months later I am still processing these life-changing words, but I continue to return to the prayer I wrote in my journal before the appointment:

> *Heavenly Father,*
> *Whatever we learn today…*
> *it doesn't catch You off guard;*
> *it doesn't diminish Your love for us.*

Whatever we learn today…
You are still bigger;
You are still in charge.
Whatever we learn today…
You can bring good from it and further Your purposes;
You are with us and for us.
Whatever we learn today,
we continue to choose to trust You.
Amen.

Time and time again we have had to *choose* to fix our eyes on Jesus. In Psalm 16:8 David writes, "I keep my eyes always on the Lord. With him at my right hand, I will not be shaken." In seeking to keep our eyes always on the Lord, we take our eyes off the challenges in front of us. In fact, if the Lord is at our right hand, then our eyes are looking to the side and not in front. I am learning it is better to keep our eyes on the Lord and to let Him guide us ahead. If we do, we will not be shaken.

Choosing to lean into community has been essential to a courageous response. It's never been easy for me to share my needs with others, but I've found the beauty and strength of community. The prayers and kindnesses of many have been special gifts that kept us going in a season that was more than we could bear on our own.

To be honest, choosing to care for myself has been challenging. After all, my wife was diagnosed, not me. She was going through much more than I was. I think I even found it helpfully distracting to focus on trying to care for Lea, the kids, and work responsibilities. However, I know much more now about the critical difference that healthy habits such as sleep, diet, and exercise make in choosing to respond with courage.

Difficult circumstances and suffering will arise in this life. Sometimes there is nothing you can do to prevent it. But you do have a choice in how you will respond. You don't control the outcome. Instead, you can choose to entrust every challenge to God. He can bear your every burden. As Psalm 55:22 says, "Cast your cares on the Lord and he will sustain you." Trusting God and responding with courage starts with making a daily decision to walk in the light, keep your eyes on Jesus, lean into community, and take care of yourself. To live and lead courageously as Jesus did, you must rest in the truth that Jesus is with you and leading you, while depending on the Holy Spirit to fill you with courage.

Reflection Questions

1. If Jesus faced significant challenges, does that reframe your perspective on your challenges? How?

2. What gifts or blessings have you received in difficult times? What gifts or blessings are possible to receive in the midst of difficult times?

3. What can you do today to fix your eyes more on Jesus? Do any of the choices listed apply to you today? (The choices listed were: Choose to Walk Toward the Light, Choose to Fix Your Eyes on Jesus, Choose to Lean into Community, and Choose to Care for Yourself.)

4. Navigating alone is dangerous, so who can/do you lean into for support?

5. What do you need to entrust to God? (Pray: God, I choose to entrust You with _____.)

6. In what way do you need to respond with courage today? This week? This year? Ask God for the courage you need.

7. Who could you give courage to today? Reach out. Pray. Write a note. Make a phone call. Come alongside. There are people all around you who need the encouragement.

A Prayer

Dear Lord,

My fortress, my strong tower, my strength.

Thank You for Your courage in the face of infinite suffering.

You didn't give in or give up no matter what, so neither will I.

By Your grace, I choose to keep my eyes on Jesus—dependent on Him rather than focused on my own inadequacy.

I choose to trust You and follow Jesus rather than be paralyzed by my fears.

I choose to keep my mind focused on Your goodness rather than be dominated by negative thinking.

I choose to press on with Jesus in courage, even when it might be easier to give in or give up.

May all who are watching me see that I am ordinary on my own but more than a conquerer with Jesus.

I pray these things in the strong name of Jesus, the lion of Judah.

Amen.

A Prayer

8

Pursue Holiness Like Him

**For we do not have a high priest
who is unable to empathize with our weaknesses,
but we have one who has been
tempted in every way,
just as we are—yet he did not sin.**

HEBREWS 4:15

The call to holiness can stir up some pushback. For starters, in the twenty-first century, the concept of holiness can seem old-fashioned or worse. Few people talk about holiness, unless they are making fun of people who act like party poopers. Right and wrong seems to be more and more dependent on an individual's own choice, feelings, and desires.

It seems as though the norm is to do whatever we want, when we want, with whom we want.

Even if we embrace the notion of holiness, the thought can quickly seem like an impossible pipe dream this side of heaven. Some people feel ashamed and trapped by their own sin. There's a sense of despair and defeat rather than hope for holiness. Others argue that since everyone messes up, why is holiness a big deal? After all, there are worse things going on the world than what we might be doing; and, since the cross of Christ covers it all anyway, why get uptight about it?

But holiness matters—it is core to God's character. Jesus lived a life of holiness and died on the cross that we might be made holy. Though Christ's sacrifice ultimately makes us right with God for eternity, we are called to pursue holiness in our earthly life. Our holiness is part of God's intention from creation. Holiness allows us to walk in freedom, to bring joy to God, and to be fully engaged in God's work. Our holiness also helps others see God. Hebrews 12:14 says, "Without holiness no one will see the Lord." By being set apart, other people take notice. They see someone and something that is different. This difference can draw people toward God.

The pursuit of holiness isn't optional for Jesus followers, although we sometimes treat it as though it is. And the pursuit is hard. Temptations abound, starting with the battle waging within us. Apostle Paul writes, "Although I want to do good, evil is right there with me. For in my inner being I delight in God's law; but I see another law at work in me, waging war against the law of my mind and making me a prisoner of the law of sin at work within me. What a wretched man I am!" (Romans 7:21–24).

Added to our internal battle is an adversary who is adeptly skilled at handcrafting lures designed to tempt and trap. According to

1 Peter 5:8, "Your enemy the devil prowls around like a roaring lion looking for someone to devour."

There are two slippery slopes that lead to deep ditches when we think about the evil one. The first slippery slope is to see the evil one behind every challenge and every turn. This slippery slope leads to a ditch that gives him too much credit. This thinking can also lead to paranoia. The way to avoid this ditch is to live out 1 Peter 5:8 where Peter says, "Be alert and of sober mind." In other words, we need to be aware, to be watching, and to keep in mind that we have a very real enemy. But remember, we also have a God who is much more powerful.

The other slippery slope we can take is to dismiss the reality that there even is an evil entity who is actively working against God's purposes in us and the world. Very early on, Jesus faced the evil one head on. Right after the beautiful experience of His baptism where He heard life-giving words from His heavenly Father and the Spirit descended on Him, the tables quickly turned. Mark 1:12–13 tells us that, "At once the Spirit sent him out into the wilderness, and he was in the wilderness forty days, being tempted by Satan."

We can only imagine the breadth, depth, and strength of these temptations. It was a subtle, yet full-on assault to undermine the precious words of truth Jesus had just been told. It was a direct attempt to leverage the vulnerability of Jesus while He was alone and isolated in the desert. The evil one's goal was to derail Jesus' entire mission before it even began.

The wilderness temptations unfolded over forty days. Jesus was fasting to focus His heart, mind, and spirit on the Father. Yet, fasting can stir vulnerability on multiple levels, and the evil one saw and seized this opportunity. He first challenged Jesus by saying, "If you are the Son of

God, tell these stones to become bread" (Matthew 4:3). The obvious temptation is the sustenance of bread. After forty days, some bread would have met a very real hunger pain. However, there was a deeper temptation centered on the evil one's first word *if.* "If you are the Son of God" contradicts exactly what the Father spoke over Jesus at His baptism. Did Jesus really believe that He was God's Son? Did Jesus have an inner need to prove it? Could He be triggered on a dare to perform a trick in order to meet His own physical needs?

Jesus didn't bite on the Enemy's lure of bread. He chose to set aside His own physical needs. He chose to lean into His true identity as God's Son. He didn't trade His long-term mission for the temporary satisfaction of a loaf of bread that would have met a short-term need and derailed what He was called to do. Instead, Jesus chose to step away from the trap to impress others, and He embraced who His Father said He was. God's Word was Jesus' foundation as well as His greatest weapon. He responds, "It is written: 'Man shall not live on bread alone, but on every word that comes from the mouth of God'" (Matthew 4:4).

The rest of the passage records two more temptations. Both are strategic, subtle, and geared to derail and destroy Jesus and His mission, but He is both alert and of sober mind. Though the temptations are real, He sees the traps for what they are. Again, He refutes them by declaring God's truth. Then, we read, "Then the devil left him, and angels came and attended him" (Matthew 4:11).

We know the devil left the desert at that point, but he didn't ultimately give up. Jesus was the evil one's highest value target. If Jesus could be derailed, then there would be no cross, no defeat, and no salvation for anyone. But rather than seeking to escape from these temptations, Jesus continued to choose holiness and to bring transformation to the world.

Jesus experienced every temptation known to human beings. As Hebrews 4:15 says, "For we do not have a high priest who is unable to empathize with our weaknesses, but we have one who has been tempted in every way, just as we are—yet he did not sin." Whatever your temptation, Jesus understands. He's been there. And He overcame.

Even at His darkest moment, as Jesus faced the final choice to embrace the agony of the cross, He didn't cave in or conform to the ways of the world. Instead, Jesus chose to take the Father's way. As Tim Keller puts it, "In the dark, with nobody looking, knowing that he is called to do the hardest thing anyone has ever done, Jesus still does the right thing. He does the same thing in the dark and in private that the next day he will do in full view."[26]

By being "without sin," Jesus was and is set apart. His obedience and holiness positioned Him and only Him to bear all our sins on the cross with the ultimate goal being that we might die to sin and live in righteousness (1 Peter 2:24).

Being centered on Jesus means following Jesus in obedience and holiness. You are to be set apart from sin and free to be wholly devoted to God's glory and purposes. But how do you follow Jesus when there is not only a battle waging within, but a battle being waged against you? How do you live out holiness in a culture and world that subtly, and often boldly, entices the opposite?

One belief that undermines holiness is that we can do whatever we want without consequence, all because of the cross, but this distorts the entire purpose of the cross. Jesus didn't die to give us a free pass to keep on sinning. The "free pass" idea overlooks God's heartfelt desire to protect us and provide for us. When we choose to sin, we are not only rejecting God's truth, we are also choosing to step outside of God's protection and provision. Sin is opposed to God's very character. Sin also always damages us and others. God hated sin pre-cross and He hates sin post-cross. There are simply no free passes for sin.

Sometimes we can be lulled into thinking that our sin is private, but sin is never private or without consequence. It never is. For starters, sin impacts us. Sin can literally kill us, and you can be sure that it will always cause some form of damage. It pulls us away from freedom and toward bondage. Then there's guilt, shame, and consequences. Sin leaks out of us and impacts others. It creates a rift and separation in our day-to-day relationship with God.

What we think might be private sin has a real impact on others. For instance, the "private sin" of pornography will impact how a person thinks about and looks at other people in real life. It can quickly become a tyrant with a stranglehold of control. It can affect our relationships, how our minds and bodies work, and hinder our pursuit of holiness.

It's important and sobering to remember that all sin will eventually become known—none of our sin will escape God's notice. What is not made known in this life, will be made known in the day of judgment that is coming. What may not be addressed now will be addressed later. There's no free pass. The only defense is what Jesus has accomplished on the cross.

In our pursuit of holiness, it is important to remember the collateral damage of sin. We often look at it as an isolated event. However, the initial sin is often like the epicenter of an earthquake. It is the starting point, but the damage ripples out—sometimes far and wide, depending on the magnitude of the sin. We can't fully comprehend the layers and levels of ripples or collateral damage. I often think the evil one gets more pleasure out of the ripple effect than the initial sin.

The Enemy delights in collateral damage and stirring isolation, shame, masks, and a sense of powerlessness. In contrast, God seeks to redeem mistakes and untangle the mess of sin. God is the God of miracles who can bring life, hope, healing, and forgiveness out of the darkest events and spaces. God is in the business of rescue and redemption. With God there is always an offramp exit available from the darkness of shame and the power of sin. To live in obedience and holiness, it's important to take a wider view when faced with temptation. Temptations can be very powerful when experienced in specific moments. You can become consumed and feel powerless in those individual moments. But when you look beyond the moment and refocus on the bigger view of what's happening, blessed hope and courage is restored. This wider view, as Titus 2:11–14 says:

> The grace of God … teaches us to say "No" to ungodliness and worldly passions, and to live self-controlled, upright and godly lives in this present age, while we wait for the blessed hope—the appearing of the glory of our great God and Savior, Jesus Christ, who gave himself for us to redeem us from all wickedness and to purify for himself a people that are his very own, eager to do what is good.

Every person has real and deep needs. Each of us is hardwired with needs to be loved, to feel valued, to belong, to connect, to feel safe, and the list goes on. They are all legitimate needs. However, behind every temptation is a counterfeit offer that falsely claims it can satisfy our felt needs. The offer often claims it can satisfy us faster and better than any other source. Though it may look promising upon initial glance, the counterfeit doesn't deliver, ever.

In fact, those deeper needs can become more and more acute because they aren't being addressed. By this, I mean that the negative repercussions of sin, such as guilt, shame, and powerlessness, distort the reality that satisfying our real need cannot be accomplished through sin. The key to meeting our legitimate needs in legitimate ways starts with choosing God and His ways.

In the pursuit of holiness and standing against temptation, we cannot impress or attempt to earn our way with a holy God. Jesus' finished work on the cross is the only currency we have with God. We cannot and will not succeed by our own ability and strength. We need God's help and God's strength. This means abiding in Christ and relying—sometimes moment by moment—on the unfathomable power of the Holy Spirit in us. You likely can't break free on your own, but you can with Christ who is in you and for you.

Holiness is our calling in a world where temptations abound. Being Jesus-centered means resisting temptation and choosing to pursue holiness. As Henri Nouwen writes, "The long, painful history of the church is the history of people ever and again tempted to choose power over love, control over the cross, being a leader over being led. Those who resisted this temptation to the end and thereby give us hope are the true saints."[27] Let's be hope givers by resisting temptation and pursuing holiness.

Reflection Questions

1. Why does holiness matter? (See if you can list at least five good reasons.)

2. Are you more likely not to see the evil one where he's working or to think you see him working when he's not? How do you seek to be alert but not give him too much credit?

3. Can you think of any examples in your life where you seek to meet legitimate needs in illegitimate ways? If so, does this work?

4. Materialism, sex outside of marriage, and power are three common temptations. How are you tempted in these areas? How do you seek to pursue holiness and guard from sin in these areas?

5. What is your best advice for resisting temptation and pursuing holiness instead? Why?

A Prayer

Holy God,

Thank You that You are holy through and through.

You are set apart and completely pure.

Forgive me for minimizing holiness or seeking holiness as a badge of honor.

Forgive me for giving in to temptations, rather than pursuing holiness.

Search me and know me. Show me if there is any offensive way in me.

Create in me a pure heart.

Set me free by Your power.

Sanctify me by Your truth.

Strengthen me through Christian community.

Protect me from the evil one.

May I be set apart for Your glory and for my best, so others see You.

I pray these things in the holy name of Jesus, who frees me from condemnation and gives me new life.

Amen.

9

Find Rhythms Like Him

"Come to me,
all you who are weary and burdened,
and I will give you rest.
Take my yoke upon you and learn from me,
for I am gentle and humble in heart,
and you will find rest for your souls.
For my yoke is easy and my burden is light."

MATTHEW 11:28–30

Frazzled. Frenetic. Frayed. Fatigued. Fog.

Too often, these kinds of words describe our head and heart space. After all, these words easily breed in an always on, always busy, and always connected world. When there are nonstop competing demands, constant and chaotic changes, complex decisions to navigate, plus never-ending opportunities to get distracted, it follows that we find ourselves scattered, unfocused, and eventually worn out.

The consequences of a 24/7/365 nonstop approach to living creates burdens we were not made to carry and demands we were not made to fulfill. Instead of moving too fast for too long, we must seek margin. Good things happen when we establish margin. As author Matt Keller writes, "Everything good in life, including teachability, lives and grows in the margins. And an unhealthy pace eliminates the margin in our lives."[28]

Many people point to a "perfect life balance" as the answer. The idea is that if we can keep all the balls in the air and keep juggling them at the right pace, then we will experience a sense of peace, control, alignment, and margin. Perfect life balance sounds amazing, doesn't it?! For years, I have imagined what it would be like to find it for myself. I have dreamt about finding a deep sense of tranquility, accomplishment, and even special connection with God through balance. I told myself that all I needed to do was get all the roles and responsibilities of my life in perfect alignment and equilibrium. But I've found that perfect life balance is ever elusive.

After reflecting on my failure to achieve perfect life balance for more than a few brief moments at a time, I have come to believe the problem isn't me, it's finding perfect balance. As a result, I have said goodbye to perfect balance and realized I should've said goodbye to it a long time ago.

Let me share three reasons why I have come to this conclusion:

First, I do believe balance is essential. Balance is essential for gymnastics, unicycling, tightrope walking, financial statements, diets, and many other things. However, in our increasingly complex, ever more chaotic and rapidly changing world, I don't think perfect life balance is possible. The ground is shifting too quickly for anyone to find enduring balance.

Second, I don't think perfect life balance is even biblical. The first disciples weren't pursuing balance when they left their nets to follow Jesus. Jesus wasn't advocating for balance when He called His disciples to deny themselves and pick up their crosses daily and follow Him. Furthermore, I don't see John the Baptist, Paul, or anybody else in Scripture living out or preaching perfect life balance.

Lastly, when I look at the life of Christ, I don't see Him frantically juggling His commitments to achieve perfect life balance. As a result, Jesus was never frazzled, frantic, frenzied, or foggy. He is present to His Father and to people, even in—especially in—the busyness and messiness of His daily life. God wasn't a "ball" Jesus juggled amongst many other competing balls. Jesus was connected and attentive at all times to His heavenly Father. He was sensitive and present with people. He was "all in" and focused on His mission.

Instead of pursuing perfect life balance, Jesus lived out a rhythm of being fully engaged and then withdrawing to rest and restore. We see this over and over again in the Gospels. For instance, in Mark 1:21–34, we discover that Jesus had an incredible day. He started by teaching in the synagogue and freeing a man of an evil spirit. Then, Jesus visited a friends' mother-in-law and healed her. That evening the whole town gathered at His door and many with various diseases were healed and many demons were driven out.

By anyone's standard, that's quite a day! Invigorating, unforgettably intense, and likely spiritually, emotionally, and physically exhausting. The next morning, after everyone woke up, they began to look for Jesus. After that miraculous night, everyone probably hoped to see Him perform even more miracles.

In verse 35 we read, "Very early in the morning, while it was still dark, Jesus got up, left the house and went off to a solitary place where he prayed." Jesus took time to pull Himself away. He knew He needed solitude to catch His breath, to give thanks, to enjoy intimacy with the Father and Spirit, to process what had happened, to guard His heart from the expectations and praise of others, and to listen closely for whatever the Father was calling Him to next. He took time to reflect, refresh, and refocus.

When Peter eventually found Jesus, Peter didn't find a frazzled, frenetic, frayed, or fatigued Savior lost in a mental fog. Instead, he found Jesus with great clarity, surprising focus, and deep confidence. Jesus replied, "Let us go somewhere else—to the nearby villages—so I can preach there also. That is why I have come" (v. 38). For Jesus, His next steps were clear, and He was ready to lean into His calling, even though the direction may have surprised or even disappointed some.

Pulling away for prayer and perspective wasn't a one-time practice for Jesus. Rather than pursuing perfect life balance, He practiced sustainable rhythms that would provide and protect the life He was called to live. This different kind of life is what we were created for. This different kind of life is far superior to what we might imagine perfect life balance would provide. A life of Jesus-centered, sustainable rhythms can radically and positively change your head and heart space. It can help you be present with God and people. It can bring greater focus, energy, and joy to your life and service with God.

Rhythms and rest are part of God's greater design. Think about how God has punctuated time by establishing day and night. He rested after six days of creating. There's rhythm built into creation. There is a rhythm to the four seasons each year. In the Old Testament, God ordained special celebrations for His people. He established a weekly rhythm of Sabbath for worship, rest, and delight. These rhythms create a cadence that not only sustains life, but actually brings more life.

Saying goodbye to the pursuit of a perfect balance doesn't at all diminish the importance of self-care. Your relationships, maintaining healthy boundaries, limiting commitments, stewarding physical health, establishing good time management, having fun, and practicing Sabbath are still important. Embracing Jesus-centered, sustainable rhythms will actually help you to better engage with these important areas. You can practice them knowing that Christ is present, interested, and desiring to be in the center of all you do—especially in the busyness, intensity, imbalances, and messiness of life.

One of the reasons we can often feel frazzled, frenetic, frayed, or fatigued comes from our own doing. Many of us wear busyness as a badge of honor. We can get an adrenaline buzz from constant activity. We imagine others might see us as more important. We can wrongly imagine that God might like us more if we get more accomplished. We can view the discipline of rest as a waste of time or an unattainable luxury. Maybe the most deceiving notion is that the pace of our life will somehow change one day. In reality, most things don't change for the better without intentionality.

If you want to begin establishing some new rhythms, it's best to start small. This way you are not overwhelmed by trying to start too many new patterns at once. Then, you can evaluate whether or not the new rhythm helps to keep you centered on Jesus. You can assess whether the new rhythm creates space and margin or helps you be more present with people. You can determine whether or not it adds positively to your life, focus, and energy. If a rhythm isn't working or you simply want to change things up, you can always change things up!

Since your personality, preferences, lifestyle, and season of life are unique to you, you will need to test out and see what works for you. To get you thinking, let me share some ideas for restorative rhythms.

These ideas are not a prescription that you must adopt. They are simply ideas for you to consider and get you thinking.[29]

Spiritually Restorative Rhythms

Jesus often went off to be alone with God. He longed to enjoy rest and intimacy in the Trinity. If we are to experience true rest and intimacy with the Trinity, we need this same rhythm. A few ways of resting in God include meditation, gratitude, and reflection.

When you meditate on God's Word, it gives you the opportunity to clear your mind of busyness and all the problems and struggles of the day—only then can you refocus on who and what truly matters. One way you can deeply meditate on God's Word is by choosing a passage of Scripture per week. Read it every day and focus on a new aspect of it. Throughout the day, go back to the passage in your mind and reflect on the truth of it and how it applies to your life.

Practicing gratitude is another way you can implement spiritually restorative rhythms. The simple act of thanksgiving can positively change your heart and mind. Before each meal and throughout the day, you can reflect on who God is and what He has done. At the end of each day, try to replay the day in your mind and look for at least three ways God has worked and you have seen blessing. Writing down and praying this list back to God will stir gratitude within your heart, help you to spiritually restore, and change your outlook.

By the end of the day I find that I am often carrying emotional, mental, or practical burdens into my "rest" time. I know that taking this weight into the night, even subconsciously, will hinder my rest and won't help anything. So, at the end of the day, I reflect on the burdens I am still carrying and surrender them to God. I often pray an end of day prayer adapted from A New Zealand Prayer Book. It goes, "Lord, it is night after a long day, what has been done has been done, what has not been done has not been done, I entrust all to you."[30] Since I almost always don't complete everything on my schedule, this prayer surrenders to God all that is not done and frees me to fully rest.

Some other ideas for simple, spiritually restorative rhythms include:

- Taking five minutes of silence and prayer as you start your day, ideally before screen time.
- Pausing at lunch to read a verse or passage of Scripture and pray it back to God.
- Booking a half or full day at a local spiritual retreat center or quiet space.
- Meeting regularly with a Christian spiritual director, mentor prayer partner, or small group.
- Establishing a weekly Sabbath to rest, enjoy God, and savor His good gifts.
- Identifying burdens you're carrying into the night and entrusting them to God. Saying simple prayers such as, "God, I choose to entrust _____ into Your good care."

Physically Restorative Rhythms

Believe it or not, movement can be restorative. You don't need to become an ultra-marathoner to benefit from physical rhythms. Our bodies were made for motion. We weren't made for just sitting around. When we move, we are taking care of our bodies and giving them the rhythm of movement to maximize our health.

The flip side of moving is resting. Most of us need to sleep more than we actually allow ourselves. Sleep isn't a waste of time; it's vitally important. Endless studies powerfully demonstrate that our sleep, both the quality and quantity, is incredibly important to our health and everyday effectiveness.[31] A sleep deficit reduces efficiency, impairs judgment, diminishes creativity, clouds thinking, and increases susceptibility to illness and disease. Many people struggle with sleep, but it is worth the effort to work toward solutions to those struggles.

There are many practical tips and helpful techniques to help us sleep, but we shouldn't forget that there are also a number of important spiritual realities:

- We are designed by God to require sleep.
- Sleep is a reminder that we are not God. God doesn't need to slumber or sleep (Psalm 121:4), but humans need sleep to refuel and regain strength.
- When we sleep, we are forced to relinquish control. In this act, we have the opportunity to choose to trust God to watch over all the pieces of our lives. As David wrote in Psalm 4:8, "In peace I will lie down and sleep, for you alone, Lord, make me dwell in safety."

Mentally Restorative Rhythms

Former U.S. Defense Secretary and former Chairman of the Joint Chiefs of Staff Colin Powell led at the highest level and served in many challenging roles and situations. In extremely stressful settings, Powell regularly made incredibly difficult decisions about complex problems that literally impacted the lives of thousands of people and entire nations.

One way he learned to cope with the pressure was by tinkering with old Volvos. After a long day in difficult meetings or even after commanding wars, he would break for an hour and tinker with his cars.

Spending time working on a carburetor would help clear his mind, give him a sense of accomplishment, and allow him to return to his role with renewed focus and energy.[32] It's easy to think that hobbies or sports are a distraction or waste of time. But Powell's example reminds us that by incorporating mentally restorative rhythms in our life, we can actually be renewed for success in our main roles.

After sharing about restorative rhythms with a ministry leader, I asked him if he had his own version of a "Volvo" rhythm or activity that restored and renewed him. He quickly responded that his life and ministry were too full. He claimed he just didn't have time. I followed up and asked if he could remember back to a time when he did have one and if it was helpful to him. He replied he used to play the trumpet, but he'd gotten so busy that the trumpet was in a case buried in a closet at home. I encouraged him to dig it out, get his musical chops back, and create some space for the trumpet again.

Six months later, I asked him about his trumpet. A big smile came across his face. He had dug it out and started practicing again. He went on to share that he was now a member of two musical bands—one with a group of churchgoers and one with people who likely wouldn't step inside a church. He was playing the trumpet again and using it to take time to rest from his role in leadership, while also using it to connect with new people outside the church. Overall, he had become happier and better in his role as a ministry leader.

Vacations can be another important mentally restorative rhythm to be utilized. The research is clear and overwhelming on the positive benefits of taking annual vacations.[33] It's mind-boggling how many people still choose not to take vacation time—or miss the point and stay plugged into work while on vacation.

I remember asking a newly married pastor what he did for vacation in his second year of marriage. He looked down and said things were so busy and challenging at his church, he didn't take any vacation. I then asked him what he did the year before for vacation. His answer was the same; he was just too busy to rest and restore. I was frustrated at his response. At the time, we had young kids at home, and Lea and I didn't have the freedom to go for a simple walk around the block without calling (and paying for) a babysitter. I was saddened by the thought of this newly married pastor with no kids, having great freedom, but being too busy to enjoy it. To help change this pattern, I challenged him to see the benefits of practicing a rhythm of restoration. Then, I encouraged him to get a vacation booked as soon as possible.

When I connected with this pastor six months later, I asked if he had taken a vacation. A big smile flashed across his face. He said he and his wife had taken one and that they had an amazing time. In fact, it was so good, he had already booked another vacation. Then, he made a comment I loved: "My wife thinks that my meeting with you is the best thing ever." Before he took my advice, she was probably beginning to wonder if she would ever have time away with her new husband.

Vacations don't need to be luxurious cruises in the Mediterranean. They can be simple and low cost. The point is to be intentional in developing a rhythm of restoration. Get your vacation dates set and approved six months or more in advance and post it on your calendar. If you don't set the time aside, you often won't take the time. And there is something to be said for the planning that goes into your vacation. Last-minute vacations are simply not as intentional, and you likely won't benefit as much from them. Plan and schedule time for your restoration and rest. Give importance to it.

Work Restorative Rhythms

Not everyone has control over their workday or schedule. But, if possible, you should exercise all the control you can. Too many people start their workday by simply reacting to their circumstances within their role, such as reacting to the needs of others or reacting to troubleshoot problems. It's easy to slip into reaction mode. However, to maximize your impact and well-being, it's critical to be proactive and establish rhythms that help you to maximize your contribution.

Start by asking yourself, What is the highest and best use of my time? In other words, what is it that you contribute that only *you* can contribute? Or, what is the most important thing you are paid to do? If you can clearly determine what your greatest contribution is in the workplace, then you can begin to intentionally create space and rhythms that allow you to make your *best* contribution. With your contribution clear, next, determine when you are at your best during the workday. Are you at your best first thing in the morning? Right before or after lunch? Late afternoon, early evening, or late evening? Knowing your best timeframe means you can proactively block off those times every day, or at least a few times per week, to do your most important and best work.

Understanding your best contribution and when you are at your best are two important steps to designing your ideal and most productive week. Next, create a simple five-column chart (one column for each day of the week) with ten rows to represent the hours in your workday. Use a specific highlighter color to block off sections of time for your most important work each day or each week. Then, use another highlighter color to block off regular rhythms already established within your week. For instance, I block off sections of time every Tuesday, Wednesday, and Thursday morning for one-on-one supervisory meetings and senior leadership team meetings. By proactively doing this, I no longer have to keep juggling my schedule, my team members and I all know when we will meet, and I don't have to think about it anymore.

Since my Tuesday and Thursday mornings have an internal focus, I use those afternoons to focus externally. I usually set aside Mondays and Fridays for work that requires deeper focus and concentration. Of course, my ideal week will look different than yours because we are wired differently, we have different vocations, and we are in different seasons of life. Experiment to find what works for you.

The point is to be proactive, establish rhythms, and set the pace within your schedule. There will always be surprises, distractions, and modifications to factor in. However, in the long run, if you take control and proactively establish rhythms that help you make your best contribution, you will have greater focus, more energy, and be more productive.

Here are some other simple ideas to develop work rhythms:

- I usually start my workday at my desk, then I migrate to our boardroom, and then I migrate to a coffee shop in the afternoons. Moving to a new space can feel like a fresh start and renew my energy.
- Try to combine common tasks into one focused time slot. For instance, I sign an entire batch of checks for work in one fifteen-minute sitting each week, rather than sign each time a new invoice comes in. This helps to avoid switching from one task to another over and over. Our brains don't like multi-tasking and context switching. It slows us down and drains energy.

- Don't eat lunch at your desk. Get up and go to the lunch-room or out of the office. Your mind and spirit benefit from a break.
- Leave short recovery spaces between meetings. If you go from meeting to meeting without space even to briefly recharge and reflect, your focus and energy will lag.
- Set clear boundaries around technology and connectivity. Turn off notifications, go offline to refocus, set fixed times to respond to emails, and create time limits for social media.

●

Let's take a moment to picture New York City's Central Park. If you have ever visited, you can testify to the fact that it is an incredible life-giving green space in the midst of the nonstop whir and blur of this dynamic city. There are over nine thousand park benches to sit on. There are miles and miles of paths to walk, run, cycle, and Rollerblade. There are special spaces for every sport you can think of, plus a theatre, food, an amusement park, and even a zoo.

When you look at an aerial photo of Central Park, you will see that it is completely and perfectly surrounded by skyscrapers. It's mind-boggling to consider how much money the land of Central Park might be worth to developers. City planners back in the 1800s set aside this over eight-hundred-acre parcel of land to be one of the nation's largest urban parks. Fast forward to today, and a population of over 8.5 million, you can see the foresight of the early planners. More than ever, this park brings life and restoration to people in a bustling city.

New Yorkers couldn't imagine New York City without Central Park. Their quality of life would be negatively impacted in major ways without it. The pace and speed of the city would be relentless, and there would be no place to decompress and restore. Just like Central Park, you and I need to create a special space that is set aside and protected for our own restoration.

I remember listening to an interview on a podcast with Al Andrews, who leads an organization called Porter's Call. In reflecting on the state of leaders, he said, "Most leaders are living like New Yorkers without a Central Park."[34] The consequences of a nonstop and relentless pace are enormous. We need to follow Jesus' lead and adopt sustainable rhythms where we are fully engaged yet leave space to pull back and withdraw. There are tremendous benefits if we intentionally create space in our lives. With these rhythms you can slow down, listen to God, hear what is going on in your soul, have fun, deepen relationships, and create memories. With rhythms like Jesus', we will live and lead out of overflow, wholeness, and joy.

Reflection Questions

1. Can you relate to feeling frazzled, frenetic, frayed, fatigued, or in a mental fog? How rare or regular are these feelings for you?

2. What's your reaction to moving from seeking perfect life balance to seeking Jesus-centered sustainable rhythms?

3. What specific rhythms do you already incorporate spiritually, physically, mentally, and during work? What is helping? What isn't helping?

4. What are some new ideas or next steps for further developing your spiritual, physical, mental, and work rhythms?

5. How does the Central Park metaphor of creating and guarding rhythms and space for restoration speak to you? How could this help you be more centered on Jesus and bless your life?

6. What, if anything, is holding you back from developing restorative rhythms?

A Prayer

Patient God,

Thank You that Jesus was not frazzled or frenetic.

Thank You that He modelled a life of beautiful intimacy with You, was attentive to people, and was focused on His mission.

Please forgive my misplaced attempts to run my life without stop or pause, often without space for You or the gifts You desire to give me.

Please forgive me for the times I have worn busyness as a badge of honor.

Help me to develop rhythms that center my life on Jesus, steward my time and energy, deeply connect me to people, bring life and joy, and most of all, bring glory to You.

I pray these things in the name of Jesus, the One whose yoke is easy and whose burden is light.

Amen.

Develop Like Him

"Go and make disciples of all nations,
baptizing them in the name of the Father
and of the Son and of the Holy Spirit,
and teaching them to obey everything
I have commanded you."

MATTHEW 28:19–20

A couple of years ago I was invited to a very special birthday party. It was the one hundredth birthday party for an amazing man named Evon Hedley. Evon was a mentor to me and many others over his lifetime.

Evon's party was unforgettable. The room was full of men and women he had intentionally walked alongside as a mentor and developer. I met a wide range of people, such as an investment banker, pastors and ministry workers, newlyweds, a NASA researcher, a doctor, and a young man who was also named Evon (his father named him after his mentor). One after another, each mentee took the microphone and shared about the significant impact Evon had made in their lives. I am pretty confident this sharing became the best workshop on mentoring and developing others I will ever attend. Evon lived out the priority of developing people. We were his legacy. This legacy was multiplying well beyond Evon's dreams as his mentees, in turn, helped to develop others. Then those people would hopefully continue to develop others after them. And on Evon's impact goes.

Evon didn't come up with this priority on his own—he was simply following Jesus' example. If you do a time audit of the Gospels, you will find that Jesus spent far more time developing His twelve disciples than doing anything else—it was His biggest priority. Though He was very engaged in the pressing daily demands of His ministry, Jesus spent the majority of His time intentionally investing in a few for the sake of the many.

Jesus lived with His disciples. He prayed, modeled, loved, taught, corrected, and empowered them. He used real-time training experiences, He encouraged them, and He served alongside to develop them. Jesus' investment in them was the foundation they needed to continue on and even multiply the mission beyond their leader.

Developing people was central to Jesus' life and the call to make disciples was core to His mission. Therefore, developing and discipling people is at the core of having Jesus at the center of our lives. If you don't have a formal leadership role or title, you might be wondering if this even applies to you. I believe it does. Being Jesus-centered means influencing and developing others regardless of your role, title, or job status.

Many people don't feel qualified or equipped to mentor someone else. You can even feel disqualified from investing in others because of issues in your own life. If this is you, let me encourage you. You don't need to reach perfection as a starting point to help someone else. It is really important that you have integrity between your words and actions, but what is more important is that you point people to Jesus and His way, His life, and His truth.

One significant challenge related to developing people is discerning *who* you should be investing in. A helpful tool to help you identify who to invest in, influence, and develop is based around the four Ps.

1. Prayer: Ask God whom you should be investing in, then listen and respond.

2. Proximity: Who are the people around you right now? Who has already been entrusted to your influence and care? The list is likely longer than you think. Maybe it's a team or small group at your church, or someone who reports to you. Maybe it's your kids or kids in a Sunday school class. Maybe it's your niece or nephew. Maybe it's a newer believer. How could you more intentionally develop the people already in front of you?

3. Priorities: For your team or organization, where do you most need help now or in the future? What is lacking? Who could help meet these needs with some intentional development? For your family and friends, who is in a season or at a stage in life that is challenging and may need help?

4. Potential: Who has potential that is just waiting for development? Don't just look at a surface level or for potential clones of yourself. Who is faithful, available, and teachable? Remember, it may be the people who challenge you and cause headaches who have the greatest potential. These people may just need to be refocused and polished.

It's important to remember that Jesus often chose to invest in what the world would likely call misfits and questionable characters. Jesus took great joy in seeing God glorified and seeing His mission move forward through a motley crew. As Philip Yancey writes, "From such a ragtag band Jesus founded the church that has not stopped growing in nineteen centuries."[35]

The next key step focuses on *how* you intentionally develop others. Again, Jesus is our best guide—His heart and practice is clear and compelling. To no surprise, Jesus' approach was picked up by the apostle Paul and my mentor, Evon. Let me share seven principles present in Jesus' ministry that are simple, practical, profound, and can be lived out by each one of us.

Principle #1: Love People

Jesus powerfully demonstrated love to those He was developing. He deeply cared for the disciples, He lived His life with them, and He taught the gospel to them. They didn't know Jesus from a distance—they knew Him up close. Of course, the ultimate demonstration of His love was laying down His very life for them at the cross.

This same principle is found in Paul's love for the Thessalonians. You can't read his letters without knowing that Paul sincerely loved these people. He demonstrated this love by caring for them, by sharing his life with them, and by sharing the gospel with them. As Paul writes, "Just as a nursing mother cares for her children, so we cared for you. Because we loved you so much, we were delighted to share with you not only the gospel of God but our lives as well" (1 Thessalonians 2:7–8). If you can picture a loving and tender mom caring for her newborn, you have a picture of Paul's heart toward the Thessalonians.

Evon wonderfully lived out this principle of love in his interactions with me. Beyond simply feeling his love, he would speak it to me. Every time we met, he would say, "Steve, I love you and I'm proud of you." Those words carried so much meaning and so much weight for me—so much so that I saved several of his voicemails and never erased them.

It might seem pretty basic, but we can miss loving the people entrusted to our influence and care. We can get too focused on ourselves. We can miss loving people because we are too busy getting things done or focusing on a goal. We need to ask ourselves, Am I really showing and speaking love to the people God has entrusted to me? Am I expressing love like Jesus did? To use Paul's words, Am I expressing love like a mother's care? Am I investing significant time with those I am developing? Do they know me up close or just from a distance? Am I seeking to see them like God does?

Principle #2: Pray Regularly

Jesus prayed regularly for and with His disciples. Jesus' prayer in John 17 just before His arrest and departure from His disciples is a beautiful and powerful example. Jesus' heart for His disciples is for their protection and unity. Verse 11 records Jesus praying, "Holy Father, protect them by the power of your name, the name you gave me, so that they may be one as we are one."

Paul followed Jesus' example and prayed for those he was developing. He recognized that real, deep change is grounded in God's work and forged by intense prayer. Paul begins his letter to the Thessalonians with, "We always thank God for all of you and continually mention you in our prayers" (1 Thessalonians 1:2). Notice the words "always," "all of you," and "continually." They are pretty inclusive, ongoing, and intense.

Every time I interacted with Evon, he would say, "Steve, I pray for you and the ministry every day." I am beyond thankful for the beautiful and powerful gift of Evon's prayers over the years. I am certain that these prayers shaped and helped me in ways I cannot imagine.

We can be so focused getting things done or moving a plan forward that we neglect to pray for the people around us. Do the words "always" or "all" or "continually" reflect the intensity of your prayers for those you are developing? I am both convicted and inspired by Ajith Fernando's words, "I have come to believe that praying for those I lead is the most important thing that I do as a leader."[36]

Principle #3: Be an Example

Jesus modeled the way for the disciples in every way. He was holy and sinless in the midst of powerful and constant temptations. He loved people compassionately, sacrificially, and boldly. Even if it meant tough love or watching followers walk away, He stood His ground in the face of great and ruthless opposition. He prayed and enjoyed fellowship with Father and Spirit. Jesus spoke truth, stood for justice, broke down barriers, and built bridges. His primary focus was on doing His Father's will, He embodied the kingdom values He proclaimed, and He served and finished His mission despite great personal cost. This list is in no way exhaustive, but it reminds us that Jesus is "the way, the truth and the life," not just through His words, but because of His example through actions (John 14:6).

Paul challenged the people he was developing to follow his example. He knew people would evaluate his words by his actions. He also knew that more is often caught than taught. Recognizing that his own life's example had a profound impact, Paul writes, "You are witnesses, and so is God, of how holy, righteous and blameless we were among you who believed" (1 Thessalonians 2:10).

This is a tough one. It makes you wonder what others are picking up through your example. Does your life and your example stir others to growth? Is there anything about your example that you don't want others to catch? It's incredibly important for your walk to match your talk. Your message or mission may be incredibly important, but it will be hampered or even rejected if your example doesn't stand up to scrutiny.

Evon's one hundredth birthday party was really a celebration of him finishing well. He had lived with integrity and intentionality his entire life. In fact, at one hundred years old, he was still mentoring others and serving in his local church! Evon's example spoke loud and clear. To this day, his example inspires me to follow in his ways.

Principle #4: Provide Perspective

A hallmark of Jesus was how He would give fresh—and often contrarian—perspective. The teachers of the law heard blasphemy as Jesus forgave a man his sins, healed people, and demonstrated His divine authority. When He was criticized for eating with sinners and tax collectors, He cast the vision for His mission. Jesus didn't come for the healthy and the righteous, but for the sick and the sinners. To people who wanted to keep the Sabbath rules, Jesus showed that helping people is important *every* day by healing the man with a shriveled hand on a Sabbath. The examples keep going. Being around Jesus was a nonstop shift in perspective that pointed people to God's heart, truth, and priorities.

In the first chapter of Thessalonians, Paul reminded people who were going through a very difficult time that there was a bigger perspective. He reminded them that they were loved, chosen, led by the Holy Spirit, and role models of God's message who were talked about everywhere. He went on to remind them that the bigger story wasn't over. Their current circumstances would end because Jesus was returning.

Perspective is a special gift that all of us desperately need at times. I remember being very overwhelmed with work, family, and life. I wasn't sure what I should do, but I decided to give Evon a call. He was in his mid-nineties at this point, but his memory was as sharp as ever. I shared how I was feeling and asked him if he remembered back to similar times when he was my age. To my surprise, Evon shared he couldn't recall these kinds of times from his life. Hearing Evon say this actually gave me perspective that brought relief. I realized that, although I was consumed by my current circumstances, I wouldn't feel like this forever. In fact, Evon made me realize that I might not even remember this season when I got older. That perspective helped me to take a breath and relax. I asked Evon this follow-up question: "What would you do differently if you were in your forties again?" He said, "That's easy. I'd love people more."

Principle #5: Encourage Lavishly

It is easy to get discouraged. The challenges of life, the voices within us, and the voices around us can drain and even empty us of courage. In contrast, Jesus sought to fill people with fresh courage. As Philip Yancey writes,

> Unlike most men I know, Jesus also loved to praise other people. When he worked a miracle, he often deflected credit back on the recipient: "Your faith has healed you." He called Nathanael "a true Israelite, in whom there is nothing false." Of John the Baptist, he said, "there was none greater born of women." Volatile Peter he renamed "the Rock." When a cringing woman offered him an extravagant act of devotion, Jesus defended her against her critics and said the story of her generosity would be told forever.[37]

Paul lived out this same practice. He knew that encouragement was a key ingredient for developing people, so he encouraged lavishly. He writes, "For you know that we dealt with each of you as a father deals with his own children, encouraging, comforting and urging you to live lives worthy of God, who calls you into his kingdom and glory" (1 Thessalonians 2:11–12). Paul tapped into a deep longing that is present in all people: the encouragement and comfort of a father.

Evon's words, "Steve, I love you and I am proud of you," were life-giving words that gave me courage. I knew Evon was cheering me on and wanting God's best for me. His encouragement was fuel that helped me to keep running with perseverance the race marked out for me.

It's easy to overestimate how much encouragement we think we are actually expressing to others. It's also easy to underestimate the amount of encouragement people actually need. Whether it's your spouse, your kids, your coworker or your supervisors, there is both an opportunity and need to encourage. Imagine the impact you and I could have if the people closest to us would see us as their greatest earthly encouragers.

Principle #6: Teach

If we build a foundation of love, prayer, example, perspective, and encouragement, most people will become open and even eager to listen and learn. Jesus was continually teaching His disciples. He taught them directly through parables and answering their questions, and He harnessed opportunities through teachable moments that came up in the course of everyday life. In Paul's case, the rest of his first letter to the Thessalonians is filled with teaching on practical issues and answering specific questions in their hearts and minds.

In living out the practice of teaching, Evon carried a special hand-written card around in his breast pocket. He had written a list of all the things he wanted to pass along to his mentees. The topics ranged from personal hygiene to relational skills to leadership wisdom. Before he would meet with someone, he would take the card out and ask God for direction on a topic. Over time, he would work through the topics and share wisdom and teaching.

Maybe you don't have a list of things you want to pass on, but you can take advantage of the many great resources already out there. With your team or family, you could read a relevant book, listen to a podcast, or watch a TedTalk together and then discuss. The format can be as simple as encouraging each person to bring one important insight and one question to discuss when you meet together.

Principle #7: Empower

Jesus sent out the twelve disciples to participate in and practice what they were learning and seeing Him do. He knew that experience was a great teacher and that some things are best taught through experience. In Matthew 10:1, it says, "Jesus called his twelve disciples to him and gave them authority to drive out impure spirits and to heal every disease and sickness." He gave them clear instructions and goals. He empowered them even though there were real risks and they faced the possibility of failure.

By releasing His disciples, Jesus had to give up control. However, by giving up control, Jesus opened the door for learning and multiplication. Consultant and psychologist Henry Cloud says in his book *Boundaries for Leaders,* "Great leaders do the opposite of exercising control over others. Instead of taking all the control, they give it away."[38]

I can think back to a number of people in my own life who took a risk and gave up their control to empower me to learn by doing.

Sometimes I still wonder what they were thinking when they let me do certain things. Yet, I am forever thankful that they gave me the freedom to try on my own. At times, I needed a gentle push and sometimes my knees were knocking with the challenge before me. But these were shaping experiences that helped me to learn about myself, engage new skills, and grow in character, confidence, and courage.

As you look back over these seven principles, you will notice you don't need a Ph.D. to do any of them. The encouraging news is that developing others doesn't need to be complicated or even require formal education. It does, however, need to be intentional.

A wise mentor once told me that as a pastor, he made it a goal to never go anywhere alone. He always tried to bring another person along with him. He wanted to be intentional by sharing life and ministry, as well as providing opportunities to build relationships and allow space for real-time learning. Simply inviting someone to accompany you allows others to see how you handle yourself and introduces them to new people and situations. It can also create great windows of learning, discussion, and debrief.

Recently, I made a list of the people God has used to develop me over the years. I was surprised at how many names I wrote down. Family members, teachers, colleagues, professors, church friends, bosses, coworkers, pastors, peers, coaches, mentors, and more all made the list. I am so thankful for each name on that list and for how God has blessed me through each person.

Follow Jesus' lead and seek out opportunities to develop others around you. My prayer is that these seven principles lived out by Jesus will help you be more intentional in developing others to center their lives on Jesus for God's purposes and glory.

Reflection Questions

1. What do you think Evon was thinking and feeling as he listened to his mentees at his one hundredth birthday party?

2. Who are you currently investing in? Who could you help develop? Work through the four Ps if you need help figuring out who to invest in.

3. Reflect on the seven principles Jesus, Paul, and Evon lived out. Which ones would you say you are living out? Which one or two could you take to the next level? Here's the list again: (1) Love People, (2) Pray Regularly, (3) Be an Example, (4) Provide Perspective, (5) Encourage Lavishly, (6) Teach, and (7) Empower.

4. What are 2–3 next steps for you to be more intentional in developing others? Are there any ideas from the practical idea list that you want to implement?

5. Who has helped to develop you? Create a list and consider writing a thank you note. Share the difference they have made and give some specific examples or stories. These notes can be deeply meaningful, and they often arrive at a much-needed moment. (If the person has already passed from this life, consider writing the note to the person's family, e.g., "I want to thank you for sharing your mom with me.")

A Prayer

Lord, thank You …

for each of the people who have helped to develop me;

for Jesus' example and priority as a people developer; and

for giving me opportunities to develop and disciple others.

Please show me who You want me to invest in.

Give me a love for these people. May I see them and love them as You do.

Stir my heart in prayer for them.

Remind me that I am an example, and that people are watching.

Help me to give perspective that points people to You and Your perspective.

May everyone who interacts with me have more courage.

Guide me in sharing truth and wisdom.

Use me to develop others who will go beyond my ministry and multiply Your impact.

I pray these things in the name of Jesus, the great developer of people.

Amen.

Part III

Leading More to Jesus

Jesus at the center of your life means seeking God's kingdom purposes and priorities.

11

Seek His Kingdom

"Seek first his kingdom
and his righteousness
and all these things will be given
to you as well."

MATTHEW 6:33

After a long night of unsuccessful fishing, Peter was tired and discouraged. Jesus had died just days before, and Peter had watched. He had also turned his back on Jesus. In His crucible moment, Peter deserted Him and denied knowing Him not once, but three times. Then suddenly, in Peter's lowly state, Jesus appeared.

Now, just as He did during the storm on the lake, Jesus intervenes and changes everything. And before long, Peter and the other fishermen caught more fish than they could haul into the boat. And just as He did during the storm on the lake, Jesus speaks into Peter's life in a powerful way—He directly addresses the shame Peter carried from his betrayal before Jesus was crucified.

Jesus then goes on to restore Peter and commission him to take care of His sheep. Peter is to feed and take care of Jesus' followers and join Him in building His kingdom on earth. In John 21:19, Jesus concludes His commission to Peter with, "Follow me!" The same words He first spoke to Peter are also some of the last. Jesus wanted Peter to follow Him to the ends of the earth—even to death—seeking and building His kingdom.

As we seek God's kingdom and His purposes and values, we take on the role of becoming "kingdom seekers." As Jesus taught, "But seek first his kingdom and his righteousness" (Matthew 6:33). Kingdom seekers have unique characteristics. To paraphrase Christian statesman and author Leighton Ford, kingdom seekers are focused on God's cause, they speak God's truth, accept God's outcomes, wait for God's timing, and pursue God's glory.[39] Kingdom seeking starts with recognizing and submitting to the one and only true King of kings. This is central to embracing Jesus at the center of our lives.

In order to be kingdom seekers, we first need to know the King's purposes and values, which we get a vision of on one Sabbath day when Jesus is handed a scroll to read at the synagogue in Nazareth. The Scripture passage Isaiah 61:1–2 reads:

> The Spirit of the Sovereign Lord is on me, because the
> Lord has anointed me to proclaim good news to the
> poor. He has sent me to bind up the brokenhearted,
> to proclaim freedom for the captives and release from
> darkness for the prisoners, to proclaim the year of the
> Lord's favor.

After rolling up the scroll, returning it, and sitting back down, Jesus said, "Today this scripture is fulfilled in your hearing" (Luke 4:21). That would have been a "goosebumps down your spine" moment if there ever was one. The kingdom of God was nearer than anyone thought or expected. It was right in front of them in the person of Jesus! And God's heart and purposes were going to be proclaimed and realized through the ministry of Jesus.

These prophetic verses provide a few powerful descriptors of the King's heart. They point to God's purposes and values. Good news, freedom, recovery, healing, vision, justice, and blessing are *all* desires of God's heart. These are at the core of seeking God's kingdom and bringing God glory.

The cross of Christ provides the most powerful demonstration of the King's heart. Through the cross, God calls people from one reality to another. Through the cross, God calls people from separation to relationship, from isolation to community, from selfishness to service, from darkness to light, from despair to hope, from toil to purpose, from death to life, from defeat to victory, and the list goes on.

As kingdom seekers, it's important to recognize that God's kingdom is upside down. In other words, God's kingdom and His purposes and values are radically different than the values of the world.

In Jesus' day, the concept of a kingdom was primarily based on the Roman Empire. The Romans were an oppressive power and overwhelming force that governed by authoritarian and often ruthless rule. The Jews longed for the promised Messiah who they believed would overcome the Romans and bring freedom to the people.

However, for many religious people of the day, Jesus didn't talk or act like the anticipated Messiah. He didn't try to rally the Jews to overpower the Romans. In fact, He rarely said much of anything about the Romans. He affirmed that taxes owed to Caesar should be paid to Caesar, and He even paid His own taxes.

Instead of painting a picture of a kingdom conquering a military power, Jesus painted the picture of the kingdom of God. At first glance, the picture looks as if it is upside down—the values the world holds dear are very different from His own.

People Matter

To seek God's kingdom, we need to prioritize people the way Jesus did. He was often surrounded by crowds, but the Gospels provide example after example of how Jesus connected with and cared for individual people. Most were not people the world would label as "important" or the "power brokers" necessary to help a movement forward.

Examples abound, but let's look at just a few snapshots. There's the snapshot of Jesus offending the religious authorities because He was having dinner at Levi the tax collector's house (Mark 2:15). However, Jesus eating with a man who did Rome's dirty work and likely sought dishonest gain wasn't the only incident involving tax collectors. Jesus was also eating with many other despised tax collectors and sinners who were Levi's friends.

Then, there's the snapshot of Jesus calmly and authoritatively bringing freedom and peace to a naked, scary, and extremely violent man from the town of Gerasa. There's the snapshot of Jesus spotting a despised tax collector named Zacchaeus up in a tree and inviting him to share a meal. There's the snapshot of Jesus embracing children and rebuking His disciples for holding them back from Him. There are snapshots of Jesus treating women with special care and respect that was absent from society. There are many, many more snapshots of Jesus with the sick, the poor, and those whom society would deem outcasts.

I know God doesn't have favorites, but if He did, then more than a dozen of His favorites live across and just down the street from my office. They sleep in battered tents next to the road and regularly push grocery carts overloaded with all sorts of items past my window. None would have dreamed of living like this. The path to life across the street is often paved by unspeakable wounds from life that combine with poor choices and broken social support systems. Most aren't able to work due to addiction, mental illness, or other challenges. Without work, they have little money. With little money, they can't afford housing in our overpriced and limited housing market. Without housing, an extremely difficult cycle becomes even harder to break.

I shared earlier that my family and I had been volunteering with a ministry that serves these favorites. In the midst of serving, I have experienced Jesus in fresh, rich, and real ways. I remembered how Jesus was completely at home with people on the margins. He knew the value of each person and loved each person. Whenever we serve, the ministry leader prays this kind of prayer over the people being served:

> God loves you. God cares about you. You have a place with Him, and you have a place here. If you've done something wrong, He can forgive it. If you are sick or hurting, He can heal. If you can't see a way, He can help you find a way. If you haven't seen your kids or your family, or you are lonely, know that God is near. God can give you hope that things can change because He can change things.

In Jesus' upside-down kingdom, *every* single person matters. He does indeed love wealthy people in big fancy houses, but He went out of His way to prioritize people with limited power or privilege. He cares deeply about people of color who face ongoing racism and oppression that is embedded into everyday society and historic systems. He longs to see justice and reconciliation. He cares deeply about people who may feel alone and vulnerable in nursing homes, hospitals, and group homes. He cares deeply about people in jails and halfway houses who need hope. He cares for people with special needs and challenges, as well as their caregivers. He sees people on the streets and in shelters who need compassion and practical help. He cares deeply for the poor, for immigrants, and for refugees who need resources and hospitality. He sees the widows and orphans who need special care and attention. Jesus' care for people is why being centered on Him means being a kingdom seeker who prioritizes people, especially people on the margins.

Everyone Has a Role

Another special feature of God's kingdom is that everyone has a role to play. Everyone has a contribution to make. In other words, there is no tiered system where a few special people are part of God's mission and everybody else gets to watch and cheer from a distance.

In God's upside-down kingdom, every Jesus follower plays an important role in the mission and work of God. Unfortunately, many Jesus followers, especially those without a formal title or not in vocational ministry, often feel left out or second class. They struggle to connect the dots between seeking God's kingdom and their Monday to Saturday everyday lives.

In North America, it's easy to view the Church as a group of people gathered together on a Sunday within a building. Without a doubt, the people of the church do need to gather together. However, we also need to embrace the reality of the church scattered. The church scattered encompasses the one hundred plus waking hours you spend on the front lines of your neighborhood, work, school, and communities every week.

This means that what you do Monday to Saturday really matters! In Jesus' upside-down kingdom, you have an important role to play to advance His purposes and values. This starts with seeing whatever you do—whether working, parenting, being a student, a neighbor, a family member, a volunteer, or social media user—as an opportunity to seek God's kingdom. As Paul writes in 1 Corinthians 10:31, "So whether you eat or drink or whatever you do, do it all for the glory of God."

Your work matters. Reframing your job as something you do to glorify God and serve others can be revolutionary. As author and speaker Beth Moore writes, "The same job subjected to Christ's authority can yield entirely different results."[40]

Everyday stuff carries eternal weight in God's kingdom. Doing your job or role well, in order to benefit others, matters to God. Treating your employees and coworkers fairly and generously matters to God. Being honest with your customers and vendors matters to God. Making corporate policies that are just and fair—both locally and globally—matters to God. Acting out of care for God's creation matters to God. Posts to social media that are kind and shine light matter to God. Generous giving of time, talent, or treasure matters to God. Being a considerate neighbor, inviting a lonely friend to dinner, using your voice to speak up for others, praying for others, and spending time to encourage your kids all matter to God. Jesus delights in these kinds of things.

This means Jesus followers need to recognize that even on the calmest day, God's kingdom purposes are way bigger than any one person, any one church, or any one organization. No matter how big, smart, strategic, disciplined, or well-resourced, no one can do what needs to be done on their own. Collaboration and cooperation need to be the rule, not the exception, for God's people.

Let's take this principle and get practical. Who could you collaborate and cooperate with to seek God's kingdom? Could your small group at church serve together in some way? Could your company partner with your customers and vendors to participate in the work of a nonprofit organization? Could you advocate with people of color or indigenous people facing racism or injustice? Could you make a connection between people who have the same heartbeat for service? Could you share resources, expertise, or contacts you have to help others progress? Could you speak well of other Jesus followers and ministries in your area rather than see them as competition? Could you and Christian neighbors dream up some ways to serve people of need in your community? When you pass by a church, ministry, or Christian-run business, could you pray for them?

For Jesus to be the center of your life and focus, we need to become kingdom seekers, not empire builders. This means seeking God's heart alongside other believers and serving together to further His purposes for His glory.

Reflection Questions

1. Does Jesus' mission to bring good news to the poor, freedom for prisoners, sight for the blind, hope for the oppressed, and the proclamation of God's favor inspire you? How?

2. What hinders you from being more of a kingdom seeker?

3. Where do you see people on the margins? Are you already responding or, if not, what are some next steps you can take to respond?

4. Why is collaborating and cooperating important for kingdom seeking? In what ways is this happening in your life? What are some practical ways you could work more with others to further God's purposes?

A Prayer

Let's close this chapter by praying the Lord's Prayer from Matthew 6:9–13:

> "Our Father in heaven,
>   hallowed be your name,
>   your kingdom come,
>   your will be done,
>   on earth as it is in heaven.
>   Give us today our daily bread.
>   And forgive us our debts,
>   as we also have forgiven our debtors.
>   And lead us not into temptation,
>   but deliver us from the evil one."

We pray these things in the name of Jesus, the one true King.

Amen.

12

Point the Lost to Him

**"For the Son of Man came to seek
and to save the lost."**

LUKE 19:10

I can be a slow learner. Recently, I was on a ladder trimming a tall hedge
with an electric power trimmer, and as I sliced away at the hedge, I ended
up slicing through the extension cord. Sparks flew. I was okay, but the
extension cord was done. I felt stupid and frustrated as I headed to the
hardware store to purchase a replacement. When I finally got home, I
plugged in the brand-new extension cord and climbed back up the ladder. Literally, within ten seconds or less, there were sparks everywhere. I
had sliced through the second extension cord. I couldn't believe myself!
Going back to the hardware store and spending more money on another
one seemed silly or worse, so my wife suggested I borrow a neighbor's

extension cord. I decided to take the rest of the day off yard work and not ruin somebody else's cord.

I think God has understanding and patience because many of us are slow learners. The Old Testament in particular contains story after story of the Israelites relearning the same lesson over and over. I think God's knowledge of this human fault is why Luke 15 has three parables that repeat the same point, and that is: lost people matter to God.

This phrase, "lost people," may make you cringe. It may seem offensive or at least a hyperbole. To say that somebody else is lost might seem like arrogance, judgment, or labeling. You could even argue that it is presumptive to assume there is a right way or only one way to God. After all, the argument goes, who really knows? And, what gives me the right to say otherwise to people I know, respect, and appreciate, especially when I'm not perfect? Why not just leave the "lost" word out? Instead, we could just say that people— all people—matter to God. These questions find their answer in Jesus' parables found in Luke 15.

As Jesus gets ready to tell these stories, there are a bunch of Pharisees and teachers of the law hanging around. They are offended by Jesus and they start muttering about how He "welcomes sinners and eats with them" (Luke 15:2). The root of their angst is a deeply held belief that a religious teacher should not have anything to do with unclean, unrighteous, and sinful people.

Jesus' response to their muttering is a parable about lost sheep. Though there are ninety-nine sheep accounted for, the shepherd relentlessly searches for the one that is lost. When it is found, the shepherd "joyfully puts it on his shoulders and goes home. Then he calls his friends and neighbors together and says, 'Rejoice with me; I have found my lost sheep'" (vv. 5–6). The lost sheep mattered. It was precious to the shepherd.

Then Jesus drives home the point: "I tell you that in the same way there will be more rejoicing in heaven over one sinner who repents than over ninety-nine righteous persons who do not need to repent" (v. 7). Notice the stark contrast between the joy of the shepherd, the rejoicing in heaven, and the muttering of the Pharisees and teachers.

Then Jesus shares the second parable. A woman has lost one of her ten silver coins. She carefully searches for it and when she finds it, she calls her friends and neighbors together. She rejoices. Then Jesus drives home the point: "In the same way, I tell you, there is rejoicing in the presence of the angels of God over one sinner who repents" (v. 10). The single coin mattered, and the angels of God rejoiced. The only people muttering are the Pharisees.

In case the point isn't yet clear, or more likely because we are indeed slow learners, Jesus tells the story of a lost son. The younger of two sons asks his father for his share of the inheritance. In that culture, though this request is similar to wishing his father dead, the father graciously gives him the money. The younger son then sets off for a distant land and squanders his wealth in wild living. In other words, he blows his father's hard-earned money. At the son's lowest point, now poor, he is feeding pigs just to survive. Being in the midst of pigs is clearly not a Jewish man's dream job, so the starving young man imagines returning to his father's home. His goal is to seek forgiveness and take a job as a hired servant. He wouldn't dare dream of seeking to gain back his position as son.

The younger son heads home and approaches his father's estate with anxiety and trepidation. Will he be rejected? Will he even be remembered? The response is stunning. As verse 20 reads, "But while he was still a long way off, his father saw him and was filled with compassion for him; he ran to his son, threw his arms around him and kissed him."

I know this is likely a very familiar story, but take the time to look at that verse again. His father had been watching for him. His father saw him. His father was hoping for his return; *longing* for his son's return. His father's response wasn't anger, self-righteousness, nor condemnation. It was compassion—He was filled with it. This compassion led the old man to do something he probably rarely did. He did something an older, respected man wasn't typically seen doing—he ran. Then he wrapped his arms around his son and welcomed him home.

The son apologizes and declares he is no longer worthy to be called a son. But to the son's surprise, the father immediately gives symbols to declare sonship. He calls for the best robe, a ring for his son's finger, and sandals for his feet. Then, the father calls for a feast and celebration. The fattened calf is prepared, and music and dancing begin.

Not everyone is happy, however. The older brother is so angry at his younger brother's return that he refuses to attend the party. He complains that he has been unfairly treated after his tireless and faithful service to the father. The father's response seeks to bring perspective: "'My son,' the father said, 'you are always with me, and everything I have is yours. But we had to celebrate and be glad, because this brother of yours was dead and is alive again; he was lost and is found'" (vv. 31–32).

This is now the third parable with the same point: lost people matter to God. The appropriate response isn't the muttering of the Pharisees, but a longing to see lost people reconciled to God. This reconciliation stirs the celebration of heaven and should stir the celebration of God's people on earth.

A colleague of mine shared a story once that helped me to further understand this point. The senior pastor at her former church wanted to make sure the staff understood that lost people matter to God. So, he installed a ship's bell in the office area.

His instructions were that whenever any of the staff heard a story of a lost person repenting and surrendering to follow Jesus, they were to ring the bell. That sound was the cue for all staff to drop what they were doing and gather around the bell. Once everyone was assembled, whoever rang the bell would then share the new faith story and the whole team would respond by celebrating and praying for the new follower of Jesus.

For this team, hearing the bell ring and gathering together to celebrate and pray was a powerful and tangible reminder that lost people matter to God. It was also a reminder to the entire team—from pastors to administrative staff to facilities personnel—that seeking lost people and pointing them to Christ is at the core of their calling and work together. In fact, my colleague told me that if a team member heard the bell and didn't drop what they were doing to go to the bell, then they would hear directly from the senior pastor. He would personally remind them that whatever they were doing wasn't as important as the celebration at the bell.

I don't think anybody likes to admit they are lost. To save face, most people would rather say, "We aren't lost, we are just out for a drive," or, "We haven't decided where we are going yet, so we can't be lost." Whatever our response or attempt at deflection, we can all likely relate to being physically lost. It's not a good feeling. It can be frustrating and costly. It can even be scary. If you can ever help someone who is physically lost find their way, you have done a good thing. If someone came to you and said they were going north when you knew they weren't, it would be unkind not to say something. The same principles apply when someone is spiritually lost.

At this point, you might argue that no one can be spiritually lost. It's common to hear people say that we can't know the right way, there isn't a right way anyway, or that all roads eventually lead to the same place in the end. So, we should not assume our way is the right way and just leave people to their own desires and path. In response, as we've just read in the three parables, God's word tells us that some people are, in fact, lost. Those are God's words.

It's important to highlight that the term "lost" isn't used to shame or judge. It doesn't give permission for anyone to feel superior or better than anyone else. The term is used to relate the precious value of each person to God. There's so much value inherent in each person that God sent His Son, Jesus, to "seek and save the lost."

In fact, God loves lost people so much that the central focus of His Son's mission was to die a public, humiliating, and excruciatingly painful death on the cross to provide the only way for reconciliation and restored relationship with God. Our sins—past, present, and future—separate us from God. Not only that, they put us on a collision course with a holy God. We couldn't and cannot fix this problem ourselves. Jesus was and is this way, the only way. As Jesus said, "I am the way and the truth and the life. No one comes to the Father except through me" (John 14:6). Attempting any other way to reconcile with God simply will not work.

There is an open invitation and opportunity for all to come to Jesus. As John 3:16–17 says, "For God so loved the world that he gave his one and only Son, that whoever believes in him shall not perish but have eternal life. For God did not send his Son into the world to condemn the world, but to save the world through him." Can you hear God's love in this passage? Can you see God's initiative? God's invitation isn't exclusive but open to whoever believes. The goal is to save, and the motive is love, not condemnation.

There is also a flip side to being lost, and that is being found. Beyond each lost person being found is God's desire for each and every person to live to the fullest. As John Stott so eloquently wrote:

> We must never conceive of 'salvation' in purely negative terms, as if it consisted only in rescue from sin, guilt, wrath and death. We thank God that it is all these things. But it also includes the positive blessing of the Holy Spirit to regenerate, indwell, liberate, and transform. What a truncated gospel we preach if we proclaim the one without the other! And what a glorious gospel we do have to share when we are true to Scripture![41]

God doesn't want anyone left out. He doesn't want anyone lost. He wants everyone to experience true life with Him. This is why anyone who follows Jesus is automatically appointed as an ambassador. As 2 Corinthians 5:18–20 reads:

> All this is from God, who reconciled us to himself through Christ and gave us the ministry of reconciliation: that God was reconciling the world to himself in Christ, not counting people's sins against them. And he has committed to us the message of reconciliation. We are therefore Christ's ambassadors, as though God were making his appeal through us. We implore you on Christ's behalf: Be reconciled to God.

A recent study by Barna Group found that most practicing Christians believe that part of their faith means being an ambassador. In fact, 95–97% across all generational groups agreed here. Furthermore, the study found that 94–97% believed the best thing that could ever happen to someone is for them to know Jesus.[42]

Though these statistics sound encouraging, there's a pretty big exception. According to the study, "almost half of millennials (47%) agree at least somewhat that it is wrong to share one's personal beliefs with someone of a different faith in hopes they will one day share the same faith. This is compared to a little over one-quarter of Gen X (27%), and one in five boomers (19%) and elders (20%)."[43]

It used to be true that Jesus followers didn't want to share their faith because they were apathetic, afraid, or didn't know how. This study shows a very different reason why emerging generations may not want to share their faith. The reason is a much deeper issue. The reason is the belief that it is actually wrong to share your faith with the hope of seeing someone of another faith embrace it.

Some argue that all faiths have similarities and are just different paths to the same destination. Therefore, the argument goes, let everyone walk on the path of their choosing. While it is really important to affirm everyone's right to choose their path, there are distinct and major differences between faiths. These differences lead the paths in different directions, which means they end at different destinations.

In other religions, there is a distinction between the leader and the teaching. The leader points you to teaching to believe and live out. In the case of Jesus, there is no difference between the messenger and the message. Jesus didn't point to a philosophy—He pointed to Himself.

Unlike any other religious leader, Jesus chose to be the sacrifice that brings reconciliation between a sinful humanity and a holy God. But the story doesn't end with Jesus dead on a cross. He overcame death and left His tomb empty. The resurrection gives powerful proof to His identity, as well as incredible authority to His teaching. Jesus is, as He said, "the resurrection and the life. The one who believes in me will live, even though they die" (John 11:25).

It may be difficult, uncomfortable, or even outright scary to share your faith in Christ at times. But it is not wrong to do so. It is actually a very loving thing to do if done respectfully and in love. It's not something we should be ashamed about. Paul writes, "For I am not ashamed of the gospel, because it is the power of God that brings salvation to everyone who believes" (Romans 1:16). Sharing the gospel can "save others by snatching them from the fire" (Jude 1:23). The gospel can positively change a life in the here and now, as well as for eternity.

God has entrusted His followers with the role of being His ambassadors and reaching out to lost people. As a result, Ajith Fernando writes, "The one who has all authority has entrusted us with a commission, and we are to proclaim this message with confidence based on his authority."[44] This is an incredible privilege and awesome responsibility. Sharing your faith grows your dependence on God, deepens your faith, and brings your faith to life.

It is amazing to consider God has uniquely placed you and me within proximity of people who may never enter a church or happen upon the gospel. These people are dear to God. They are hardwired for a relationship with Him. For myriad reasons, they don't know that Jesus is the gate to relationship with God or how to find the gate. May your example in life, your words, and your actions clearly point people to the gate.

Reflection Questions

1. What do the three "lost" parables teach you about God's heart toward people who are spiritually lost? (You can reread the parables in Luke 15 to refresh your memory.)

2. Why does God not want anyone left out of His kingdom? Why do you want others to know and follow Jesus?

3. Is it right to share your faith with someone of no faith or a different faith in hopes that they will know and follow Christ? Why or why not?

4. Are you currently embracing or hesitating in your role as one of God's ambassadors pointing people to Jesus? What's working? What's holding you back?

A Prayer

Seeking God,

Thank You for Your loving posture toward sinners—me included.

Forgive me for muttering, being distracted, and not pausing to celebrate when someone who is lost is found. May my heart always rejoice with Yours on each occasion.

I humbly embrace my role as an ambassador of Christ. Thank you for this special privilege and awesome responsibility.

Forgive me when my actions have indicated disbelief, disobedience, or even being ashamed of the gospel.

Stir me with your love, great wisdom, creativity, and courage to point people to Jesus.

May many find Jesus—the gate—and be changed now and forever.

I pray these things in the name of Jesus, the Savior.

Amen.

13

Build Bridges to Him

"Very truly I tell you,
whoever hears my word
and believes him who sent me
has eternal life and will not be judged
but has crossed over from death to life."

JOHN 5:24

The disciples couldn't believe their eyes as they approached the well. What was Jesus doing talking to a Samaritan woman, let alone one with a bad reputation? Why was He doing it? Better yet, how could He do it? Didn't Jesus know this was against all the rules? Didn't He know this would compromise His mission and further provoke the religious authorities? But building bridges was central to Jesus' life and ministry. He was constantly breaking down barriers and building bridges to connect people to God.

In John 4, we see one of many powerful illustrations of Jesus breaking down barriers and building bridges. Back then, a Jewish rabbi
wouldn't allow himself a conversation with a sinful Samaritan woman.
There were clear and long-standing cultural, racial, gender, and religious
barriers that made this interaction out-of-bounds. By simply being present, asking for some water, and engaging in a conversation, Jesus broke
down every one of these barriers. And as the conversation deepened,
Jesus built a bridge that changed the woman's life forever.

Jesus didn't just build bridges—through His sinless life, His death
on the cross, and His triumph over the grave, He *is* the bridge. He is
the great high priest who bridges the gap between humanity and God.
Being a follower of Jesus means you are also a priest. This means that
you are a bridge builder with Jesus. So, with the goal of leading more
people to Jesus, let's look at some practical steps we can take to join Him
in His mission of bridge building.

See People

A commercial from a few years ago for the Toyota Yaris makes a powerful point. It begins with a window washer working on a ladder several
stories up the side of a building. Suddenly, the ladder shifts and falls to
the ground. The window washer is now clinging to the windowsill to
avoid falling two stories.

The lady inside the apartment sees what has happened, tells the
window washer to "hold on," sprints downstairs, and rushes outside.
But rather than righting the ladder to save the window washer, the lady
gets into her Toyota Yaris (located right underneath the window) and
drives the car forward out of harm's way. With the car safely out of the
way—and even though the window washer is still holding on for his life
two stories up—she gets out of the car and heads back into the building.

The commercial closes with the words "You can love it too much," in reference to the car.

It's a funny commercial, but it's too close to reality. We can all miss seeing people—even those who are right in front of us. At times, we are too self-focused, other times we are distracted and worried by many tasks that cloud our vision from seeing what is really important.

Thankfully, Jesus saw individual people. He was constantly surrounded by crowds, but He saw individuals. Examples of this abound. Jesus didn't see the woman at the well as different, bad, or dangerous. He didn't live out the prejudice of His own tribe. Jesus saw her as a valuable person made in the image of God for a relationship with God, who had unique challenges and needs. Jesus' mission was about seeking, and saving the lost, and it starts with seeing people.

Ask God to help you to see people. Seek to be more attentive to the people He puts right in front of you. Aim to see people who are different than you through God's eyes. It's sobering to remember that we will never look into the eyes of another person whom God does not love enough for Jesus to have died for.

Get to Know Your Neighbors

A few years ago, a number of Denver-area pastors were working together to strategize how to best reach their community with Christ. As part of their research, they met with their mayor and asked how they could best help the city. After talking through a long list of urban challenges, the mayor shared that the best thing the churches could do wasn't to start or fund another program; the best thing they could do was to be good neighbors.

The simple goal of what became a neighboring movement was to empower Christ followers to live out the second greatest commandment and love our neighbors by being good neighbors. Knowing and loving our neighbors is foundational obedience to God. It's a powerful expression of God's love toward people who don't yet know or follow Him.

Sadly, according to *The Art of Neighboring*, less than 10 percent of Christ followers can name their eight closest neighbors. Less than 3 percent can provide basic facts about each neighbor and less than 1 percent can share deeper values that each neighbor holds.[45] The simple truth is that we can't live out the second greatest commandment if we don't see or know our neighbors. On the flip side, there is a great opportunity right outside our front doors. We can all begin to pay attention and prayerfully seek out opportunities to see and get to know our neighbors.

Getting to know our neighbors is often easier said than done. In my neighborhood, it's actually challenging to even physically come into contact with many of them. Many people aren't outside very much, and most drive right into their garages where, seconds later, the automatic door closes and seals them off. Many people simply stay inside and are inaccessible. That's why we need to seize opportunities when they arise. Patience, intentionality, the gift of hospitality, and prayerful creativity can all be very helpful.

Find Third Places

A number of years ago, sociologist Ray Oldenburg popularized the term "third place." He identified our homes as our primary or first place. This is where we spend the most time. Work or school is usually our second place. A third place is another environment where we interact with people more informally over time. These places are usually not hierarchical or highly structured. They are neutral ground where people can be comfortable and engage other people in meaningful relationships, conversation, and fun over time. This third place can be a local coffee shop, community club, gym, library, restaurant, sports facility, or park. Third places play an important role in connecting people and ideas.[46]

We can readily apply the concept of third places to our role as Christ's ambassadors. Too often, we expect people who don't know or follow Jesus to somehow show up at church. We have a "come to us" mentality, which is exactly opposite of Jesus' approach. His model wasn't to wait and hope for people to come to Him. Instead, He intentionally, actively, and strategically focused on seeking people out. This meant Jesus spent a lot of time in places where He would connect with those outside the synagogue.

It's easy to discount the power of third places. We may already be spending time in a third place yet not be connecting the dots between that place and the opportunity to be Christ's ambassador. Conversely, many of us spend so much time doing Christian activities with Christian people, we don't have a third place. In fact, many Jesus followers don't actually interact with many people who are not already following Him.

A third place is a natural space for you simply to be present in an ongoing way. It's a space to be prayerfully connecting with people who don't yet know and follow Jesus. This doesn't mean you are looking for ways to force every conversation toward a spiritual topic. It means naturally being the aroma of Christ through your example, actions, and words.

Do you already have a place like this? If you do, how intentional are you about being an ambassador with Jesus in this space? If you don't already have a third place, can you begin to pray and think about where you might naturally begin to frequent, spend time, get to know people, and be in their presence with Jesus?

Love People

"God is love" (1 John 4:8). His heartbeat is love. Jesus loved people.
He demonstrated love in a multitude of ways—even to people often
deemed unlovable by the world. God's love is captivating and conta-
gious. It is the greatest apologetic of our faith. Yet, people often need
to see and experience God's love and our love for them in order to hear
and respond to the gospel.

One practical way Jesus demonstrated love was by simply being
friendly, and He was particularly friendly toward people outside the
religious establishment. As Philip Yancey writes:

> He would accept almost anybody's invitation to dinner,
> and as a result no public figure had a more diverse list
> of friends, ranging from rich people, Roman centuri-
> ons, and Pharisees, to tax collectors, prostitutes and
> leprosy victims. People liked being with Jesus; where
> he was, joy was.[47]

One of my longtime friends and mentors, Dr. Dave Overholt, follows and teaches Jesus' example of being friendly. He encourages Jesus
followers to be 10 percent more friendly with the people you meet in
everyday interactions. This simple concept is actually pretty counter-
cultural. In our busy and distracted world, we often have short trans-
actions with people rather than being present and actually building
deep relationships.

Being 10 percent more friendly means taking an extra moment with
the store clerk, restaurant server, cab driver, or fellow traveler. It means
being present to them as Jesus would. It starts with paying attention
because this person matters to God. It often moves to asking a question

and then taking time to listen. Believe it or not, this simple practice can open up opportunities to naturally encourage someone, meet a practical need, pray for them, and even have deeper faith conversations. It is amazing to see what this simple but intentional change in perspective can do to build bridges and open the way for the gospel.

Look and Listen for Deeper Needs

Jesus saw past the externals. He saw people's deeper needs. He saw inside their souls. For instance, in Mark 1, a man with leprosy came to Jesus and begged on his knees that Jesus would make him clean. The man's leprosy was a physical affliction evident to everyone. This was his external challenge.

However, Jesus saw behind this man's leprosy. Jesus was filled with compassion. Why? Because Jesus understood this man's life had been defined by his disease. He was spiritually unclean in the eyes of the religious authorities and he was dangerous in the eyes of his community, and he had been rejected by both. Beyond the painful physical ailment, this man was suffering great emotional and relational pain.

It's here that Jesus does a double healing. The first healing comes as Jesus "reached out his hand and touched the man" (Mark 1:41). The man, an untouchable, was touched. He hadn't likely felt the warmth or acceptance of a simple touch since he received the disease. Jesus' touch redefined the man's identity and value. It brought emotional healing. Then came the second healing—the physical healing. Jesus said, "'Be clean!' Immediately, the leprosy left him and he was cleansed" (vv. 41–42).

It's often easy to see the external challenges people are facing, and we are to care about them as Jesus cares. But Jesus also looked past the externals to see the internal condition. People all around us—the ones

He puts in our path—are suffering from internal challenges, and He especially cares about those.

I am slowly learning this fact in my own middle-class neighborhood. When I walk our dogs around the block, I can see the externals. I can see cut lawns and nice modest homes. I can be tempted to conclude that people must have their lives together. From the sidewalk, things look okay. Therefore, I assume everyone inside the homes must be okay too.

After more than fifteen years in the neighborhood, I'm learning there are actually a lot of deeper needs that you can't see from the sidewalk. Within one block of my home, there have been three suicides, two battles with cancer, a chronic illness, two cases of infidelity that broke up both relationships and their families, a police raid, a drug house, and a neighbor who pretty much lived all four seasons in his backyard drinking beer after beer every single night. And this is only what I know about. Bottom line is, there's a lot more going on and a lot more needs than we see from a quick external look.

We shouldn't assume. Everyone has a story. Everyone has deeper needs they long to see fulfilled. Ask the Lord to give you vision to see what He sees. Keep your eyes and ears open. Get to know people. Be available to them. Listen and look for their heart cries. Above all, love people.

Remember Your Example

I once had a boss who said, "Whenever I find out someone is a Christian businessperson, I hold onto my wallet. I know they are going to try to rip me off." My heart sinks when I reflect on that statement. It's far from positive and it's based on multiple bad experiences. It's a reminder that our example and actions can either build a bridge for people to connect with God or build barriers that keep people from God.

When you are known to be a follower of Jesus, people watch. They are eager to know whether you are really different or if you are another hypocrite who talks one way and actually lives the opposite. We can't live up to a perfect ideal, but our talk should closely align with our walk. People need to see the gospel in you before they hear the gospel from you. The fruit of the Spirit should be evident in your life, and if it is, people will be drawn toward Jesus. If our actions really follow the pattern of Christ, then others will desire to follow Jesus.

Your example may need to be proven over time. This is especially the case when someone has had a prior bad experience with Christians—and too many people have had prior bad experiences with Christians. These people will need to see you live out your faith over time before they will take time to listen or engage.

Tell Your Story

When the disciples found Jesus talking with a woman at a well, she left her water jar behind, went back to her town, and began to tell her story. After interacting with Jesus, she told her community, "Come, see a man who told me everything I ever did" (John 4:29). As she told her story, people became curious. They asked, "Could this be the Messiah?" and they began to make their way toward Jesus. In other words, they were drawn to Jesus. In fact, verse 39 says, "Many of the Samaritans from that town believed in [Jesus] because of the woman's testimony."

The woman at the well simply and naturally shared about her encounter with Jesus. God used her story to draw people to Himself, and their faith grew as they encountered Jesus for themselves. As the people said, "We no longer believe just because of what you said; now we have heard for ourselves, and we know that this man really is the Savior of the world" (v. 42).

What's your story? Ironically, we can easily forget our own. Time can dim our memory and we can forget what first drew us to Jesus. We can get so immersed in the Christian life that we can forget what got us started. As I reflect back on my journey toward Jesus, I land back at a very distinct moment in time. It was the eve of my eighteenth birthday. I went to bed looking forward to celebrating this milestone. But my sleep was interrupted. My stepmom woke me up in the middle of the night. She told me that my dad was sick and that I needed to wait outside for the ambulance to arrive. To say the least, that was quite a wake-up call.

After my dad made it to the hospital, my stepmom and I were in the waiting room trying to process the surreal night. We heard announcements paging doctors and various codes being called over the PA system. We heard doctors barking orders and the sound of the defibrillator pounding off my dad's chest in the next room.

In those moments that seemed to last forever, I felt incredibly alone. I felt my world was being thrown completely out of control. The only thing I could do was pray. So, that's what I did. I prayed to the God I always believed existed but didn't really know or care much about. With tears streaming down my face, I asked God to spare my dad's life.

Thankfully, my dad came through that night. But that event became a turning point for me. God used it to connect the dots between the seeds of faith that were planted early on in my life and what I had been hearing from my youth group friends. It launched my own search to get to know God more personally and, ultimately, led me to follow Jesus.

The hospital trip adds some drama to the story, but at the heart of it are some deep universal needs: I felt alone and useless. Not many people can relate to the specifics of my hospital story, but most people can relate to the overarching themes of feeling alone and having no control. I am also convinced all people have a built-in longing to discover what I did—that I could walk every day, whatever good or bad the day might bring, with the God who is good and in control. God can use my story to connect others to Him. I simply need to share my story.

I've heard Jesus followers say they don't have a story or at least they feel they don't have an interesting one. They will explain how they came to faith very early in life and can't even remember life apart from following Jesus. Or they will compare their story with someone else's more dramatic, spectacular testimony and often sheepishly self-select out.

My response is to encourage people to focus on identifying, celebrating, and sharing what God has done for them. Your story might start when you started to follow Jesus at four years old. Your story might be about how God helped you at work yesterday. You don't have to have an "edge of your seat" narrative that encompasses your entire life. The point is to identify something significant that Jesus has done in your life, whether long ago or last week, and to share it. How would your life be different if Jesus hadn't been or done that one thing? Now look for the deeper need that God met. If you can identify the core need Jesus met in your life, your story will connect with others who have experienced that same core need.

The goal isn't to mesmerize people with the drama and details. People can easily get lost or too focused on them—they end up remembering the story but miss seeing God. The goal is to faithfully point people to Him, to who He is, what He has done, and the difference He makes in your life.

Take confidence knowing that God is actively going about His business to draw people to Himself. God hasn't given up, and we shouldn't give up either. To live with Jesus at the center of who we are, we need to break down barriers and build bridges. We need to see people, get to know people, be more friendly, love people, live with integrity, and share who Jesus is and what He has done. What a responsibility and privilege!

Reflection Questions

1. What are some reasons why it may be hard to really see people and get to know their deeper needs?

2. The book, *The Art of Neighboring,* suggests drawing a tic-tac-toe grid. This grid represents your neighborhood. Mark your home and then mark the names of all the neighbors you know around your home. Of the eight empty spots, how many names do you know? Of those names, do you know facts about each neighbor? Do you know deep values or heart cries for each neighbor?

3. Do you have a "third place"? Describe it and specify whether or not you've been able to be intentional as an ambassador with Jesus. If you don't have a third place, can you think of a place that could work?

4. Are you up for doing a one-week trial of being 10 percent more friendly? What could this look like?

5. What's your story? Identify one significant thing Jesus has done in your life. Whether you look back long ago or last week, how would your life be different if Jesus hadn't done that one thing or been there? What's the deep need that Jesus addressed in you that others might relate to?

6. Who are you not "giving up" on to come to faith? Pray for this person now.

A Prayer

Dear God, who sees me.

You see each and every person. You want every person to come to a knowledge of the truth and into relationship with You.

Thank You that Jesus is the bridge that connects people to You.

Thank You that Jesus saw people and their deepest needs.

Help me to see people, to build bridges to my neighbors, and to be Your ambassador in third places.

May my example and my witness have integrity. May my example, words, and actions point people toward You, not away from You.

Please give me opportunities to share my story of how You have made such a big difference in my life.

I ask for faith and perseverance to faithfully share the good news of the gospel.

I pray this in the name of the only One who saves—Jesus, the Savior.

Amen.

14

Pray for Others to Follow Him

"This kind can come out only by prayer."

MARK 9:29

I had never heard of anyone praying over toilet seats.

I was in Florida serving as the follow-up coordinator for Josh McDowell's speaking tour. Josh was doing a series of large youth events with a popular Christian band where the band would play several sets and Josh would share the gospel. My role, as part of my seminary internship, was to prepare the volunteers who would connect and pray with people wanting to learn more or follow Jesus.

At one particular venue, there was a prayer team assembled, ready and waiting to walk into the stadium that morning. Once inside, they physically touched and prayed over each and every one of five thousand-plus seats. Their prayer was that God would bring a young person who needed to hear the gospel to fill that specific seat. Not wanting to miss any potential spot, they told us they had also prayed for every single toilet seat!

A few hours later, the parking lot began to fill, and long lines began to form outside. The doors opened, and the stadium quickly began to come alive. Before long, every single seat was filled. To me, this seemed like a miracle. But there was also an issue arising.

The problem was that there were people lined up outside who couldn't even get in. That's when the MC went to the microphone. After a warm welcome, he shared that their prayer for weeks was that every seat would be filled with young people who needed to hear the gospel. Then he made a bold request. He asked every adult sitting in a seat to give it up and leave the building to make room. This act of selflessness, he shared, would make room for young people still waiting outside to hear the gospel inside.

After the MC repeated the call, the adults responded and began to leave, and more young people began to enter. After the first music set, Josh took the stage and began to share the gospel. At the end of his talk, he invited everyone who wanted to follow Jesus to get up out of their seats and make their way to meet our team of volunteers for follow-up and prayer.

Immediately, hundreds and hundreds of young people got up. In fact, so many began to move from their seats that Josh asked them to stop. He wondered if they misunderstood the invitation, so he explained again. Rather than deter response, more young people rose to their feet and started to move toward my team.

At the end of the night, I was reminded afresh that all people are designed for a relationship with God. Deep inside, there is a longing for Him. God takes initiative to meet that longing. He is very much about His business in drawing people to Himself.

I also learned one more important piece to the story. Remember all the adults who left their seats to make room for more young people? When the adults left, most of them didn't do what I likely would have done, which is go to a nearby coffee shop to visit with friends and kill time before returning to drive my kids home. Instead, these adults prayed. In fact, I'm told they formed a prayer ring around the outside of the stadium. I believe that their prayers were a key part of God's amazing work inside the building. Though they couldn't see the impact from their vantage point, God was very much and very powerfully at work.

This event was a profound reminder about the importance and ministry of prayer in leading more to Jesus. It's an encouragement to be intentional in prayer. It's a call to be faithful in prayer even when you can't see what God is doing from your vantage point.

Prayer was central to Jesus' life and ministry. As Luke 5:16 says, "But Jesus often withdrew to lonely places and prayed." Whether it was very early in the morning before others were awake or a special trip to the top of a mountain, Jesus longed for intimacy with Father and Spirit through prayer. He also knew prayer was critical to see the Father's purposes advance. Through prayer, we have the privilege of intimacy with God. You can know He cares about you and attentively listens to what you share. It's life-changing to know that God also desires to share His heart and perspective with us.

Beyond a privilege, prayer is also a responsibility where you can partner with God in His work in the world. If you long to see God's purposes and priorities move forward in the here and now, then prayer must be a priority. Specifically, since Jesus' mission is "to seek and to save the lost" (Luke 19:10), you can trust that prayer is foundational to God's mission.

I was recently asked this question: "If all the people you prayed for last week to come to faith did come to faith, how many people would have come to faith?" At first this sounds like a riddle of some sort. But the point behind the question is this: are you actually praying for lost people to be followers of Jesus? Then comes a second question: "If not, why not?"

These questions convicted me about my own lack of prayer focused on people coming to faith. When I reflected on my prayers from the previous week, I recognized most of my prayers were about me, my family, my work, and my stuff. The lost were lost by my nonstop focus on me.

Through praying for people to respond and follow Jesus, we have an opportunity to join Jesus at the center of His ministry. Our prayers join in with Jesus' work in powerful ways that we don't fully understand on this side of heaven.

We often mistakenly believe that prayer is how stretching is to running; it's a helpful way to get warmed up for the real work of doing ministry. Oswald Chambers overturns this faulty thinking in his classic *My Utmost for His Highest*. He writes, "Prayer does not equip us for greater works—prayer is the greater work."[48] If our desire is to be Jesus-centered, then prayer for lost people must be a priority, not an afterthought.

The necessity of prayer is why Paul tells the people in the church at Colossae:

> Devote yourselves to prayer, being watchful and thankful. And pray for us, too, that God may open a door for

our message, so that we may proclaim the mystery of Christ, for which I am in chains. Pray that I may proclaim it clearly, as I should. Be wise in the way you act toward outsiders; make the most of every opportunity. Let your conversation be always full to grace, seasoned with salt, so that you may know how to answer everyone. (Colossians 4:2–6)

The word "devote" is convicting for me. It's all-in and full-on. Paul didn't use the word "dabble." We aren't to dabble in prayer. Instead, we are to be devoted. I think Paul's vision for being devoted in prayer would have lined up well with the folks in Florida praying over every seat—including the toilet seats.

There are a lot of ways we can raise the temperature on prayer to see God's purposes advance in the world. I want to focus specifically on partnering with God's work of drawing people to Himself. More teaching and learning are always good, but sometimes we need to just do it. To this end, I have pulled together more than a dozen practical ideas to help you start praying for more people to know and follow Jesus.

- **Make a List:** One simple starting point is to make a list of three to four people you know who don't yet follow Jesus. Write these names on a Post-it or inside the cover of your Bible. Then make a point to pray for these people every day.
- **Ask for Opportunities:** You can start your day by simply asking God to give you an opportunity to share or live out the gospel in actions and words. Then keep your eyes and ears open as you journey through your day.
- **Silent Stranger Prayers:** Sometimes I pray silently for

strangers I pass by during the day. For instance, when I run in the mornings, I often pass students walking on their way to school. I sometimes pray, "Lord, I pray this student would come to know You and experience Your love for them." I may never see that person again, but I may be the only person who prayed for them that day. Maybe my prayer will join with many others who are already praying and there will be a breakthrough. Either way, I'm hopeful to one day learn about the impact of these prayers.

- **Set Specific Times:** Some friends of mine who are church planters set their watch alarms for 10:02 a.m. each day. They chose 10:02 because of Luke 10:2 which reads, "The harvest is plentiful, but the workers are few. Ask the Lord of the harvest, therefore, to send out workers into his harvest field." When the 10:02 alarm goes off, they stop what they are doing and take a moment to pray this verse. They pray for more workers and they pray for workers who would be clear, creative, and bold communicators of the gospel.

- **Revival:** You can pray for revival where God stirs fresh life, fresh focus, and fresh urgency in His people. Revival in your local church, revival through the shared ministry of churches in your city, or revival in the Church in your country. Pray for a conviction, a desire, and the boldness you need to share the gospel. Pray Colossians 4:2–6 that God would open doors to proclaim the gospel, that the gospel would be proclaimed clearly, for wisdom toward outsiders, and that the most is made of every opportunity. Pray for revival to start in your heart that it might overflow to your city and country.

- **Strategy:** When you plan special events and outreach opportunities, be sure to be intentional about a prayer strategy. Too often, all the effort goes into planning and marketing the event, while prayer becomes an afterthought. Start with prayer and remain focused on prayer. No matter how amazing the event, I am convinced there is a strong correlation between prayer and lasting impact.

- **Kid's Friends:** A dad once shared with me that every time one of his kids shared the name of a friend they were spending time with, he would write down the name of the friend and begin regularly praying for him or her. By praying for the friend's salvation, this dad was also seeking to bless and influence his own kids with friends who know and follow Jesus. Over the years, this list of friends has gotten long, but I'm inspired to hear him say that he is still faithfully praying.

- **Offer to Pray:** Remember that most people of any faith or non-faith background will not stop you from praying for them. So, when you are in conversation and the person shares a need, ask if you can pray for them right then and there. Most people are humbled and grateful that someone else would do so. This kind of spontaneous prayer plants spiritual seeds and provides an opportunity for them to see God answer.

- **Find an App:** There are many apps that can help you pray for the work of the gospel around the world. For example, Joshua Project's "Unreached of the Day" app gives basic background and prayer items for a different unreached people group each day. The "Operation World" app is another simple tool that guides you daily into having a global impact through prayer.

My hope is that a few of these ideas inspire and equip you to turn up the temperature on prayer for people to know and follow Jesus. You can become like the adults who saw an opportunity and encircled the stadium to pray from outside the conference. From your vantage point, you may not see the outcomes of all your prayers, but you can trust that God is at work and about His business of drawing people to Himself. You have both an awesome responsibility and amazing opportunity to pray for the advancement of the gospel. It's at the heart of being Jesus-centered.

Reflection Questions

1. If all the people you prayed to come to faith last week did indeed come to faith, how many people would have come to faith? How do you feel about your answer?

2. What hinders your prayers for people who don't yet follow Jesus? What helps your prayers?

3. The last section of this chapter shares a number of practical ideas to help you pray for lost people. Is there an idea that you would like to start implementing? Which one?

4. Take a few moments and start praying right now for people who don't yet follow Jesus. Identify three people or people groups who don't yet follow Jesus and pray for them now.

A Prayer

Dear Lord,

Your loving heart longs for lost people to be rescued, redeemed, and reconciled.

Stir my heart with Your heart. Forgive me for my focus on me and for my complacency.

Thank You for the responsibility and opportunity to join in Your mission through prayer.

Right now, I pray that _____ would come to know and follow Jesus.

I pray these things in the wonderful and powerful name of our Savior, Jesus Christ.

Amen.

Conclusion

Be, Live, and Lead Different

Back in 1997, a young computer company called Apple was under a great deal of pressure from the then industry giant, IBM. IBM's "THINK" marketing campaign was strong and gaining momentum. So, Apple CEO Steve Jobs gathered the best marketing minds of the day and the rest is history.

Apple's "Think different" campaign was birthed, and it charted not only a new course for the company but a new trajectory for global technology. If you have never seen Apple's first *Think different* commercial, it featured pictures of iconic twentieth century personalities. With pictures of Einstein, Ghandi, Martin Luther King Jr., Amelia Earhart, and thirteen others as the backdrop, the narration read:

Here's to the crazy ones.

The misfits.

The rebels.

The troublemakers.

The round pegs in the square holes.

The ones who see things differently.

They're not fond of rules.

And they have no respect for the status quo.

You can quote them, disagree with them, glorify or
vilify them.

About the only thing you can't do is ignore them.

Because they change things.

They push the human race forward.

While some may see them as the crazy ones,

we see genius.

Because the people who are crazy enough to think they
can change the
world, are the ones who do.[49]

Then the new Apple "Think different" tagline flashed on the screen. It was a fresh, powerful, and inspiring commercial that successfully launched the campaign that put Apple on the map. Apple has been innovating, thinking differently, and changing the world ever since.

Despite Apple's tremendous impact on our world, it's nowhere near to being in the same league with Jesus. The true key to being different, living different, and leading different is Jesus. Whoever you are and whatever you do, Jesus is the ultimate difference maker. Jesus alone can transform you into the person you were meant to be, and Jesus alone can empower you to impact not only our world but eternity.

Being Jesus-centered starts with being led more by Jesus. Taking your lead from Jesus should make a real difference in who you are, how you live, and how you lead. The goal is to become more like Jesus from the inside out. Jesus needs to be at the center, and your life needs to be centered on Him.

Jesus at the center of your life can't be a secret. God's presence and work in your life should stir a longing to seek God's kingdom purposes and values. You have a significant role to play, and you have an opportunity to make a real and eternal difference. Pointing more people to Jesus is about responding to Jesus' call—whoever you are and whatever you do—to share the good news of the gospel in love with actions and words.

Centering your life on Jesus isn't a program you complete or a book you read. It's not a box you check off. It's a lifetime pursuit. My hope is that you have been captivated afresh by Jesus through these pages. I pray that you have discovered principles and practical next steps to guide you and shape you in the future.

Jesus changes everything. For God's glory, may you be different. For God's glory, may you live different. For God's glory, may you lead different.

Closing Prayer

Dear Lord,

I'm in awe of Jesus.

I'm in awe of Jesus' life.

I'm in awe of what Jesus has done for me and all humanity.

I'm in awe of the opportunity to walk with Jesus each and every day.

I'm in awe of the opportunity to join with Jesus in His work in the world.

Though some might see me as a crazy one, misfit, rebel, or troublemaker, I want to live life differently. I want to lead differently. I long for our world to be different.

To this end, by Your ultimate power and grace, I want my life to be centered on Jesus so that I will be changed from the inside out.

I desire to be led more by Jesus as well as live and lead more like Jesus.

I want to center my life on Jesus, so more are led to Jesus, so that lives will be changed for eternity for Your glory.

I pray these things in the one and only name of Jesus.

Amen.

Acknowledgments

Writing a book is a team sport, and I am deeply indebted to several amazing teams.

I can't imagine a more amazing best friend and wife than my Lea, who teaches me daily about the unconditional love and boundless grace of God. Luke, Ainslea, and Lauren, I am wonderfully proud of each of you. Being your dad is the honor of my lifetime. Always know that Mom and I are your biggest fans.

At Arrow Leadership, I am also part of a fantastic team that seeks to wholeheartedly serve with Jesus at the center. Founder Leighton Ford's faith-filled vision and book *Transforming Leadership* has been a catalyst for changing my life and leadership, along with so many others. I will always be grateful for Dr. Carson and Brenda Pue's prayerful, encouraging, and empowering investment in me over many years.

My longtime friend, mentor, and Arrow board chair Miller Alloway has been a patient yet persistent champion to "get writing," along with a wonderfully encouraging board of directors, including Keith Anderson, Sam Chaise, Heather Cova, Peter Huizinga, Janet Johnson, Jay Lee, Aklilu Mulat, Ruth Pape, Jonathan Scott and several others over the last decade who are deeply committed to developing Jesus-centered leaders.

Day-to-day, I serve with an amazing team. From our gifted and committed staff to trainers, volunteers, and partners around the world, it is a true gift to serve with you in our great privilege of walking alongside and polishing Christian leaders! Special thanks to my leadership team—Dr. Rick Franklin, Dr. Sharon Simmonds, Dr. Taylor Williams and Tarra Wellings—who has gracefully and prayerfully served alongside me for more than seventeen years. Our Abbotsford office team do much of the heavy lifting—Alison Boettcher, Kourtney Cromwell, Dana Franklin, Zephan McMillan, Sharla Vander Woude, and Amanda Klassen—my diligent assistant who capably organizes much of my world.

Every day I am inspired by a global network of over two thousand alumni of the Arrow Leadership Program. Thank you for seeking to be led more by, to lead more like, and to lead more to Jesus. In this particular mission, your labor is by no means in vain. May God do in and through you more than you can ask or imagine.

A book would not be a book without a publishing team. Thank you Fedd Agency and the Fedd Books team for bringing this book to life. From Esther Fedorkevich's encouragement to Tori Thacher's wise and insightful editorial leadership along with Alli Harrell, to Allison East's design and attention to detail, I am grateful I had an amazing team around me. Thank you for making the process a joy!

Special thanks to everyone who invested time in providing feedback on early manuscripts and to the many supporters who have cheered me on along the way.

Where this book has come up short, please know it's completely on me. There's certainly not anything amiss or lacking in the subject of the book. In Jesus, we find the One and Only.

May your wonder and awe of Jesus keep growing day by day!

About
Dr. Steve Brown

Steve is husband to Lea and dad to three teens—Luke, Ainslea, and Lauren. Based near Vancouver, British Columbia, Steve develops Jesus-centered leaders around the world as president of Arrow Leadership.

Communicating, coaching, and creating Jesus-centered resources are Steve's heartbeat. He's the author of *Leading Me: Eight Key Practices for a Christian Leader's Most Important Assignment*, *Great Questions for Leading Well*, and free monthly e-resources at www.sharpeningleaders.com.

With experience in local church, denominational, parachurch and marketplace roles, Steve has also earned degrees from Wilfrid Laurier University (HBBA), Tyndale Seminary (MDiv) and Gordon-Conwell Theological Seminary (DMin). In addition, he's thankful to be a graduate of the Arrow Leadership Program.

You can connect directly with Steve at www.steveabrown.com or www.jesuscenteredbook.com.

About
Arrow Leadership

Our world needs Jesus-centered leaders! For more than thirty years, Arrow Leadership has focused on developing leaders who are led more by Jesus, lead more like Jesus, and lead more to Jesus.

We live out our purpose by delivering transformational programs, creating exceptional resources, and sharpening Christian leaders globally. Our heart's desire is to see Christian leaders equipped to influence every sphere of society, impact every nation, and reach every person for Jesus.

To learn more and take your next step in Jesus-centered life and leadership, please visit: www.arrowleadership.org or call 1-877-AN-ARROW. You can also subscribe to receive free e-resources at www.sharpeningleaders.com.

Endnotes

Chapter 1

[1] John Stott, *The Radical Disciple: Some Neglected Aspects of Our Calling* (Downers Grove, IL: InterVarsity Press, 2014), 20.

[2] David Elliot, *Hope and Christian Ethics*, (Washington DC: Cambridge University Press, 2017), 121.

[3] Philip Yancey, *The Jesus I Never Knew*, (Grand Rapids, MI: Zondervan, 1995), 80.

Chapter 2

[4] Ajith Fernando, *Jesus Driven Ministry* (Wheaton, IL: Crossway Books, 2002), 36.

[5] William Barclay, *The Gospel of Matthew*, (Louisville, KY: Westminster John Knox, 1975), 1:49.

Chapter 3

[6] Karl Barth, "Shocking Liberalism," *Christianity Today*, August 8, 2008, https://www.christianitytoday.com/history/people/theologians/karl-barth.html.

[7] Henri J. M. Nouwen, *Life of the Beloved: Spiritual Living in a Secular World* (Spring Valley, NY: Cross Road Publishing, 2002), 33.

Chapter 4

[8] PhilipYancey. *I Was Just Wondering*, (Grand Rapids, MI: Wm. B. Eerdmans Publishing Company, 1998), 141.

[9] Os Guinness, *Rising to the Call: Discovering the Ultimate Purpose of Your Life* (Nashville, TN: Thomas Nelson, 2003), 77.

[10] Timothy Keller, *Encounters with Jesus: Unexpected Answers to Life's Biggest Questions* (New York: Penguin Books, 2015), 144–145.

Chapter 5

[11] Dallas Willard, *Renovation of the Heart: Putting on the Character of Christ* (Colorado Springs, CO: NavPress, 2002), 105.

[12] Willard, *Renovation*, 105.

[13] Willard, *Renovation*, 105.

[14] A. W. Tozer, *The Knowledge of the Holy: The Attributes of God: Their Meaning in the Christian Life* (New York: HarperCollins, 1978), 1.

[15] John Stott, *The Radical Disciple: Some Neglected Aspects of Our Calling* (Downers Grove, IL: InterVarsity Press, 2014), 45.

[16] Stott, *The Radical Disciple*, 47.

[17] Willard, *Renovation*, 95.

Chapter 6

[18] Philip Yancey, *The Jesus I Never Knew* (Grand Rapids, MI: Zondervan, 2002), 36.

[19] Mark Buchanan, *Your God Is Too Safe: Rediscovering the Wonder of a God You Can't Control* (Colorado Springs: Multnomah, 2001), 93.

[20] Lewis, C.S., *Mere Christianity* (Grand Rapids, MI: Zondervan, 2001), 121-22.

[21] Packer, J. I., and Loren Wilkinson, eds. "Pride, Humility, and God." Essay. In *Alive to God: Studies in Spirituality Presented to James Houston*, (Vancouver, B.C.: Regent College Pub., 2000), 111–22.

Chapter 7

[22] Timothy Keller, *Encounters with Jesus* (New York: Viking, 2013), 52.

[23] Dietrich Bonhoeffer, *The Cost of Discipleship* (New York: Touchstone Publishers, 1995), 43.

[24] C. S. Lewis, *The Screwtape Letters* (London: Geoffrey Bles, 1942), 29.

[25] *Gen. George S. Patton*, in a U. S. Army Letter of Instruction (March 6, 1944); reprinted in *War As I Knew It* (New York: Bantam Books, 1947).

Chapter 8

[26] Keller, *Encounters with Jesus*, 166.

[27] Henry J. M. Nouwen, *In the Name of Jesus: Reflections on Christian Leadership* (Spring Valley, NY: Cross Road Publishing, 1989), 79.

Chapter 9

[28] Matt Keller, *The Key to Everything: Unlocking the Secret to Why Some People Succeed and Others Don't* (Nashville, TN: Thomas Nelson, 2015), 65.

[29] Ken Shigematsu, *God In My Everything: How an Ancient Rhythm Helps Busy People Enjoy God* (Grand Rapids, MI: Zondervan, 2013).

[30] He Karakia Mihinare o Aotearoa, *A New Zealand Prayer Book*, ANZBP/ HKMOA edition, (Anglican Church: Aotearoa, NZ and Polynesia, 1988). Accessed November 16, 2020. https://anglicanprayerbook.nz/.

[31] "Why Do We Need Sleep?" by Eric Suni, SleepFoundation.org, updated September 11, 2020, https://www.sleepfoundation.org/articles/why-do-we-need-sleep.

[32] McGinn, Dan, and Joe Posnanski. "A 4-Star Mechanic and the Pingpong Fanatic: Passions of Two High Achievers." bizjournals.com. Accessed December 8, 2020. https://www.bizjournals.com/bizjournals/news/2018/10/31/a-4-star-mechanic-and-the-pingpong-fanatic.html.

[33] "You Really Do 'Need' a Vacation," by Suzanne Deggs-White, PhD, *Psychology Today*, July 15, 2018, accessed November 12, 2020, https://www.psychologytoday.com/intl/blog/lifetime-connections/201807/you-really-do-need-vacation.

[34] Al Andrews, Donald Miller interview with Al Andrews, *10 Things Powerful People Can Do to Not Screw Up Their Lives*, podcast audio, October 2, 2017, https://buildingastorybrand.com/episode-64/.

Chapter 10

[35] Philip Yancey, *The Jesus I Never Knew*, 100.

[36] Ajith Fernando, *Jesus Driven Ministry*, 167.

[37] Yancey, *The Jesus I Never Knew*, 89.

[38] Henry Cloud, *Boundaries for Leaders: Results, Relationships, and Being Ridiculously In Charge*, (New York: HarperCollins Publishers, 2013), 128.

Chapter 11

[39] Leighton Ford, *Transforming Leadership: Jesus' Way of Creating Vision, Shaping Values & Empowering Change*, (Downers Grove, IL: InterVarsity Press, 1992), 98.

[40] Beth Moore, *Jesus, the One and Only*, (Nashville, TN: B&H Publishing Group, 2013), 94.

Chapter 12

[41] John Stott, *Baptism and Fullness: The Work of the Holy Spirit Today*, (Downers Grove, IL: Intervarsity, 1975), 25.

[42] Barna Group, Faith & Christianity, "Almost Half of Practicing Christian Millennials Say Evangelism Is Wrong," February 5, 2019, https://www.barna.com/research/millennials-oppose-evangelism/.

[43] Ibid.

[44] Ajith Fernando, *Jesus Driven Ministry*, 126.

Chapter 13

[45] Dave Runyon, Jay Pathuk, and Randy Frazee, *The Art of Neighboring: Building Genuine Relationships Right Outside Your Door*, (Grand Rapids: Baker Books, 2012), 39.

[46] Ray Oldenberg, *Celebrating the Third Place: Inspiring Stories about the Great Good Places at the Heart of Our Communities*, (Lebanon, IN: Da Capo Press, Hachette Book Group; illustrated edition, 2011).

[47] Philip Yancey, *The Jesus I Never Knew*, 89.

Chapter 14

[48] Oswald Chambers, "The Key of the Greater Work," *My Utmost for His Highest*, October 17, https://www.utmost.org/the-key-of-the-greater-work/.

Conclusion

[49] Galloppa, Davide. "Think Different." Think different. Original Ad. Accessed November 16, 2020, https://www.thecrazyones.it/spot-en.html.